Data M Storytelling

MW00836920

An Agile Approach to Maximizing the Value of Data Management

Larry Burns

Technics Publications

2 Lindsley Road
Basking Ridge, NJ 07920 USA
https://www.TechnicsPub.com

Edited by Carol Lehn
Cover design by Lorena Molinari
Cover derived from Giovanni Domenico Tiepolo, The Storyteller (1773)

First Printing 2021

Copyright © 2021 by Larry Burns

ISBN, print ed.	9781634629492
ISBN, Kindle ed.	9781634629508
ISBN, ePub ed.	9781634629515
ISBN, PDF ed.	9781634629522

Library of Congress Control Number: 2021939663

To Roger Paulsen, data architect and master data modeler, for all his help, support, and inspiration.

To Meg Clarkson, data architect, data modeler and Data Services Manager, who believed in me and gave me my start in this profession.

To Valerie Eikum-Skaggs, DBA extraordinaire, who started our DBIX program and has been our organization's strongest advocate of good data modeling and database design standards.

And to Donna Smith, enterprise architect and human resources specialist, who introduced me to Human-Centered Design.

Enjoy your retirements, all of you, and thanks for all you've contributed to our organization over the years.

Acknowledgments

First and foremost, I would like to thank my wife, Becky, for her interest in Native American culture and storytelling traditions, many of which I draw upon in this book. Becky has always supported my work, and her wisdom and insights have helped me greatly.

I would also like to acknowledge the continual and ongoing help, support, and encouragement of my colleagues in our organization's BI and Data Services and Enterprise Architecture groups, as well as many fine people in our various business divisions across the globe. I couldn't (and wouldn't) do the work that I do without them.

I owe a tremendous debt of gratitude to my good friend and colleague John Giles, and to Carol Lehn, for their work in reviewing my manuscript and offering their insights, comments, and corrections.

And last (but not least), I would like to thank Steve Hoberman and the wonderful people at Technics Publications for their encouragement and hard work; this book would never have seen the light of day without their efforts. You'll have to judge for yourself whether that's a good thing.

Contents

Is there such a thing as a Data Modeler Dinosaur? Have some data modelers got stuck in the past, perhaps not seeing the need to change if they want to survive? Sadly, I think so.

It's true that some of the foundations of the data modeler's craft haven't changed much. The definitions for First Normal Form, Second Normal Form and beyond have been stable for decades. And if the scope of a modeler's work focuses just on physical models for implementing relational databases, change is slow.

But it's also true that for many modelers, things have changed. "Agile" development puts pressures on us with timelines of weeks or even days to deliver models. "Big Data" doesn't always want to play nicely with past practices. Then there's "Schema-on-read". What, are people saying that we don't know the structure of data before we write it? Or heaven help us, there's talk of "unstructured" data. What's the world coming to!

They are perhaps some of the *technology* changes that practitioners encounter. But the elephant in the room reflects changes in how the *business* see us, or want to see us.

So what's at the center of this seismic shift? Many of us used to design physical databases for discrete projects. Now the call to arms is to help the business get value from their data, to position data truly as an enterprise asset. A data modeler is no longer merely a technical member of some IT team. Now, if they embrace Larry's message and approach, the data professional is a core contributor to the business itself.

I've got some good news, and some bad news.

First the bad news. If some data modelers consciously picked their career to avoid change, they are likely be disappointed, if not unemployed. Soon!

Now the good news. Larry's book has pulled together decades of hard-won experience, *and* he's thoughtfully embraced and carefully applied new thinking, and applied it to modeling. He is also one of those rare people who evaluates theories and applies them in practice. His book presents a way for us to deliver value to the business, and to be valued by the business. And to have fun along the way.

A myriad number of books exist for the purpose of explaining the various techniques of data modeling – normalization, subtyping, cardinality, modeling notations, design patterns, etc. However, there are three important questions that I think have not been adequately addressed in data modeling literature, and it is these questions that I intend to address in this book.

The first question is: *Why* should we be doing data modeling at all? For the most part, we do data modeling because we've always done data modeling, or because it's an organizational practice. As I said in my first book,[1] the younger generation of developers regards data modeling as an artifact of 1980s-era relational databases and client-server architecture. And data modeling is, in fact, very useful for designing relational database structures, especially for OLTP (transactional) applications. But in a data universe increasingly populated by non-relational, highly scalable databases, is there still a place for data modeling?

The second question is: *What* is the nature of the value that data modeling contributes, and to whom? Is data modeling merely a descriptive task of cataloging an organization's data assets, or is it (or can it be) something more useful than that? What value does the activity of data modeling contribute to an organization or to an IT project?

The third question is: *How* can we most effectively do our data modeling work in an IT world increasingly centered around Agile and DevOps practices? Traditional approaches to data modeling ("Give me your business requirements and I'll send you a data model in a month or two.") simply won't work in today's business and IT environments. But there hasn't been a great deal of research done on data management processes and the comparative effectiveness of different approaches.

As I explained in my first book, I was forced to confront these questions early on in my data modeling career, as I started doing data modeling, database design, and database development work for Agile software development projects. The developers I worked with did not believe that data modeling was value-added work (they saw it as another example of Big Design Up Front), and they weren't willing to allow data modeling work to impact the project schedule or the velocity of the project team. I needed to come up with both a *justification* of data modeling as a necessary and valuable part of the application development

---

[1] Burns, Larry. *Building the Agile Database* (New Jersey: Technics Publications LLC, 2011).

process, and a *process* for doing data modeling and other data work that dovetailed nicely with the cadence of Agile development.

Since then, the challenges facing data modelers and other data professionals have only increased. We now have an over-abundance of data persistence technologies, both on-prem and in the cloud. It is no longer necessary (so they tell us; I'm still skeptical) to design databases for performance or scalability or efficiency or data integrity or ease of use. Just cram the data in anywhere and let the applications have access to it. Of course, we've heard all this before, haven't we?[2] But modern database technologies have certainly made it less necessary than in previous eras to extract the maximum amount of performance and efficiency out of a database. And the cycle time between new business requirements and production implementation of solutions has shortened to the point where multiple deployments per day (we're doing two per day on my current project) are the new reality.

As the lead data architect/data modeler/database developer for a Global Fortune 200 company, I am on the front line of all these changes and am having to continuously adapt my practices to the needs of my ever-increasing and ever-demanding customer base. This book, the third in the series, represents the continuation of my Agile Data journey, and the development of my thinking and practice in the field of data management. I welcome your presence and your participation in this journey.

As always, I will be making frequent use of analogies and metaphors (the storytelling metaphor, for one), and will be drawing from practices in non-data-related fields (such as psychology, design theory, and engineering). As always, I will not be prescriptive in my approach (that is, I will not try to tell you exactly how you should do data modeling, or any other data work). I will try to uncover some useful principles that you can adapt and apply, as needed, to your own

---

[2] Someday, I'm going to try to figure out why every technological "advancement" seems to propel us at least 30 years into the past.

work. And, as always, the aim of this book is to help you achieve the maximum amount of success in the work that you do for others.

There are five sections to this book:

In Section I, *Data Model Storytelling*, I will talk about the nature and value of data modeling, and draw some lessons from storytelling traditions to illustrate how data modelers can interact more effectively with their audiences.

- Chapter 1 examines the nature of data modeling itself, and describes how data modeling can add value to projects in a world that is becoming increasingly non-relational.

- Chapter 2 applies the storytelling metaphor to the work of data modeling, showing how data modelers can help organizations "tell their data story".

- Chapter 3 draws some lessons from effective storytelling and applies them to data modeling work.

- Chapter 4 explores the various audiences (i.e., types of stakeholders) that data modelers interact with, and suggests the most effective types of communication for each.

- Chapter 5 describes how data modelers can act in a "Shamanistic" capacity when working with groups of stakeholders.

- Chapter 6 describes how data modelers can make data modeling a more fun and interactive experience for their audiences.

- Chapter 7 explains different types of data modeling notations, and how each can help Modelers tell a different sort of story.

- Chapter 8 explores how data modeling can contribute value to the work of Business Process Reengineering (BPR) and Business Process Management (BPM).

In Section II, *Agile Data, Revisited*, we will re-examine some of the fundamental concepts of Agile, and explore how they can be applied to various aspects of data work (Note: the material in this section is taken mostly from my half-day Agile Data workshop).

- Chapter 9 explains what Agile is (and isn't), and describes how Agile manages work so as to minimize risk and maximize opportunity.

- Chapter 10 explains the importance of architecture and design to Agile projects, and describes how to approach architecture and design in an Agile fashion.

- Chapter 11 describes Agile Data Modeling, and introduces the concept of Model-Driven Development to show the value that data modeling can contribute to Agile projects.

- Chapter 12 describes my Agile approach to database design and development, using the Object-Oriented concepts of cohesion, coupling, abstraction, and encapsulation.

- Chapter 13 describes my "pattern-based" approach to Agile BI and Analytics.

In Section III, *The Challenging Landscape*, we will examine some of the current challenges data professionals face in an ever-changing technology landscape.

- Chapter 14 explores the data modeling issues (and opportunities) around schema-less (i.e., NoSQL) databases.

- Chapter 15 explores the data modeling challenges of Domain-Driven Development (DDD), and the increasing use of microservices in application development.

- Chapter 16 examines the issue of semantics and ontologies in data modeling. Is it possible to create a semantically correct data model? And does it even matter?

- Chapter 17 explores the issue of "modeling the enterprise". How can you do this if all your modeling work is done on projects?

In Section IV, *Data Modeling and Design Thinking*, we explore the question of whether data modeling can be thought of as a Design activity. We'll examine concepts from design thinking and Human-Centered Design (HCD) to see how data modeling can help empower customers to address, and solve, problems within their organizations.

- Chapter 18 examines what Design actually is and introduces the basic concepts of design thinking.

- Chapter 19 introduces Human-Centered Design (HCD) and gives examples of how HCD techniques can help people identify and solve problems in an iterative and human-centered way.

- Chapter 20 explores how to apply HCD concepts to the process of data modeling.

Finally, Section V presents a case study illustrating the principles of this book, as applied to a fictional manufacturing company (the Blue Moon Guitar Company). This section also contains an afterword, the author's biography, a list of references and resources, a description of key terms and acronyms, and a comprehensive index.

As a bit of fun, and also to illustrate a bit of design thinking, here is a graphical depiction of the Table of Contents of this book, showing the interrelationships between the major groupings of ideas as intersecting circles, with the Chapter references in the areas where the "idea circles" intersect. This will give you a more visual overview of the book:

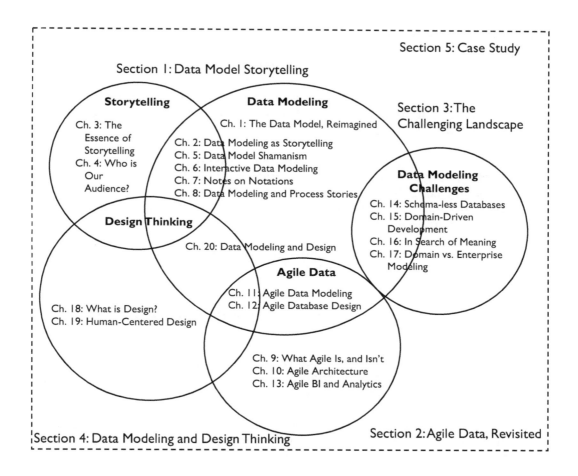

Section 5: Case Study

Section 1: Data Model Storytelling

Section 3: The Challenging Landscape

Storytelling

Ch. 3: The Essence of Storytelling
Ch. 4: Who is Our Audience?

Data Modeling

Ch. 1: The Data Model, Reimagined
Ch. 2: Data Modeling as Storytelling
Ch. 5: Data Model Shamanism
Ch. 6: Interactive Data Modeling
Ch. 7: Notes on Notations
Ch. 8: Data Modeling and Process Stories

Data Modeling Challenges

Ch. 14: Schema-less Databases
Ch. 15: Domain-Driven Development
Ch. 16: In Search of Meaning
Ch. 17: Domain vs. Enterprise Modeling

Design Thinking

Ch. 20: Data Modeling and Design

Agile Data

Ch. 11: Agile Data Modeling
Ch. 12: Agile Database Design

Ch. 18: What is Design?
Ch. 19: Human-Centered Design

Ch. 9: What Agile Is, and Isn't
Ch. 10: Agile Architecture
Ch. 13: Agile BI and Analytics

Section 4: Data Modeling and Design Thinking

Section 2: Agile Data, Revisited

Key Points

- Advocates of data modeling need to address three areas of concern: the nature of data modeling, the value of data modeling, and the process of data modeling.

- Data modelers need to address project stakeholders' concerns about whether data modeling is a value-added activity, whether data modeling contributes to the success of IT projects, and how to do data modeling effectively in the context of a project's development methodology and delivery schedule.

- Storytelling is an apt metaphor for how data modelers interact with project stakeholders to ensure that an organization's "data stories" are effectively told.

- Learning to do data modeling in an Agile fashion is key to delivering value on iterative, fast-paced IT projects.

- Data modelers also need to know how to respond to the challenges presented by constantly changing technology and ever-decreasing windows of business opportunity and expected delivery times.

- BI projects and programs face both technological and human obstacles. To be successful, technology decisions must be made, costs and risks must be managed, and human nature must be understood.

Section I
Data Model Storytelling

Stories create community, enable us to see through the eyes of other people, and open us to the claims of others.

Peter Forbes

We live in a world of stories. Every human activity and aspiration is a story – a story about who we are, what we want and need, and how we hope to turn our dreams into reality. Once we realize this, we understand (and accept) the truth of Shakespeare's immortal words:

All the world's a Stage,
And all the men and women, merely Players;
They have their Exits and their Entrances,
And one man in his time plays many parts...

We, as data management professionals, play parts in an ongoing story of how data and information are used to add value to various human endeavors. We either realize this fact, or we do not. If we do not, we will fail to recognize opportunities for our characters to advance the purpose of the story and to support the efforts of the other actors on the stage. We will be moving aimlessly around the stage while the audience ignores us, and the story continues on without us.

Once we understand this, we will learn to support the story and its characters rather than against it. Every actor learns to understand the purpose and intent of the story being presented, what the author of the story wishes to communicate to the audience, and what purpose each character contributes to the telling of the story. Every actor, every character, exists for the purpose of moving the intent of the story along and supporting the other characters who are doing the same thing. Every actor needs to learn both his or her "lines" (that is, the specific things that his/her character is doing to advance the story) and also the "cues" that he or she will give to or receive from other characters as the story moves along. Every actor learns to keep one eye on the stage, and one eye on the director.

In data management, the "story" (or "play") is usually a project of some sort. The intent of the story is to deliver content of some value to an audience (usually business people). The characters are all the people working on different aspects of the project, in different supporting roles. The director is usually a project manager or scrum master. The director's "direction" takes the form of sprint goals, user stories, and task or work assignments. The director "blocks out" the movement of the actors (project team) on the stage, makes sure each actor understands his/her lines and cues (user stories and tasks), and ensures that the interaction of the actors advances the purpose (goal) of each scene (sprint).

In this section of the book, we will explore what the storytelling metaphor can tell us about how we, as data management professionals, should view (and do) our work. I'll be introducing some useful concepts from my experiences in Toastmasters (the International public-speaking organization). And we will explore the various parts (roles) that we and the rest of the supporting cast play in advancing the story.

Chapter 1
The Data Model, Reimagined

It's about knowing what you have. The challenge is that most organizations don't know what they have.

Rosario Mastrogiacomo

The traditional Entity-Relationship data model is derived from the 12 Rules (13, actually) of relational database theory espoused by E. F. Codd, and these rules, in turn, derive from the branch of mathematics known as set theory. Which is to say that the following E-R model:

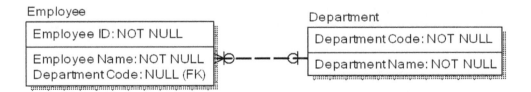

is equivalent, mathematically, to the following Venn diagram:

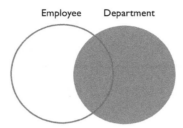

Employee   Department

Or, to express the relationship verbally, "An Employee may (or may not) be associated with one (but only one) Department, while a Department may contain zero, one or many Employees."

An E-R data model expresses relationships between sets of objects (called *Entities*) and describes the characteristics (*Attributes*) of each object set. This same relationship could also be expressed in Hierarchical form, as follows:

Employee:

- Employee ID: required, number
- Employee Name: required, string
- Employee Department:
    - Department Code: optional, string
    - Department Name: optional, string[3]

THE PURPOSE OF DATA MODELS

However rendered, data models, properly understood and properly used, are intended to perform the following functions:

---

[3] Notice that, in the context of Employee, Department Name is optional, while in the context of Department it's required. This is an example of why modeling the business data rules is important, even when the implementation of the data is non-relational.

- They are a visual depiction of the way people think (and talk) about real-world objects and the relationships between them.[4]

- They are used to test and validate assumptions made about these objects and relationships. For example, is it really true that an Employee can exist without being assigned to a Department? Can a Department exist without any Employees in it?[5]

- They guide and encourage discussions about the objects and relationships. For example, isn't there more than one type of Employee? Does each type of Employee have the same relationship with Department?

- They help surface differences of opinion about what the objects (or their attributes) actually represent. For example, different business units might have different definitions of the term "Employee". Are Contractors "employees"? Are Temps?

- They iteratively refine our evolving understanding of the data landscape associated with a business problem (or opportunity), giving all stakeholders a common basis for discussion and keeping them "on the same page".

- They help enforce common standards and definitions of data, so that data can be properly integrated and used across an organization to support various data-based business processes and initiatives.

- They can suggest possible uses and applications of the data (for example, customer-focused cross-selling and up-selling opportunities,

---

[4] The data model itself is not as important as the *conversations* the data model promotes.

[5] The most important thing a data modeler does is ask questions. Data modeling is not about drawing, it's about questioning.

or possible re-engineering of business processes to improve efficiency). Business users ought to be able to look at a data model and say, "You know what we could do with this data?"

- They also suggest opportunities to *create* new data entities, attributes, and relationships (instead of simply describing ones that already exist). It's important to remember that data modeling is as much a creative discipline as it is a descriptive one.[6]

- They guide the process of physically instantiating the data in some way (in a database, for example), as necessary to support software applications and business processes.

Another way of expressing this is that data models help a group of people "think through" the data aspects of a certain business problem or business opportunity, allowing them to surface and resolve disagreements about data meanings, explore data opportunities, design and create data resources in support of business initiatives, and achieve consensus about data meanings. In other words, a data model tells a *story*, and the story is about how a group of people come together to use data to solve a business problem (or take advantage of a business opportunity). The data model becomes *a record of the journey* from the conception of the problem to its solution.[7]

When viewed in this light, it becomes clear that data modeling has a higher-valued purpose than being simply a description of the implementation of data in some sort of database. Thus, the value of data modeling transcends the type of technology used to instantiate data. Steve Hoberman, in his excellent book *Data*

---

[6] More on this topic in due course.

[7] In one sense, a data model tells a story (like a book); in another sense it helps other people tell a story (like the script for a play).

Modeling for MongoDB,[8] points out that even when the target data structure is a non-relational, schema-less database, there are still fundamental questions of data design that need to be asked and answered:

- What does a given entity or attribute mean, in business terms? Do all business stakeholders agree with this definition?

- In what business domain(s) does an entity or attribute exist? Where and how is it managed in the business?

- What sort of data values do we expect to be associated with a given attribute?

- What sort of relationships exist between various data entities? As shown above, even hierarchies are an expression of relationships between two or more data entities.

- What business rules constrain the relationships between entities or the values of attributes? (Even though these rules and constraints may not be enforced in the database, they must be understood and consistently enforced in the application, for the protection of the business.)

- What common, organizationally-defined and frequently-used sets of data should be defined as master or reference data (and thus reused across multiple documents and data stores)?

- In which hierarchy level will we define and store a given piece of data?

- What sorts of design issues need to be understood, discussed, and resolved before creating a data store for this data?

----

[8] Hoberman, Steve. *Data Modeling for MongoDB* (New Jersey: Technics Publications LLC, 2014).

Steve's book makes the additional point that, since schema-less databases will accept any data given to them, under any name, it becomes even more imperative to make certain that everyone involved (business stakeholders, database developers, application programmers, QA testers, etc.) have a common and shared understanding of exactly what the data is, how it is defined, what it is called, and where and how it will be stored.

Here is another illustration of this important aspect of data modeling.

THE INFAMOUS "TIMESHEET" EXAMPLE, REVISITED

Readers of *Building the Agile Database* will remember the example of a "database" that some developers at one of our divisions built for a timecard entry application for division engineers. The database table looked like this:

TASKS

TaskID	IDENTITY	not null
TaskTitle	varchar	null
TaskDesc	varchar	null
ProjectNo	int	null
ProjectMgr	varchar	null
EmployeeNo	int	null
EmployeeName	varchar	null
WeekNo	tinyint	null
EstHours1	smallint	null
ActHours1	smallint	null
EstHours2	smallint	null
etc, etc, etc…	smallint	null
EstHours7	smallint	null
ActHours7	smallint	null
OvertimeHours	smallint	null

The point I made in the book was that this data "design" violates the business's understanding of what a timesheet (or timecard) is and the business rules that constrain timesheet data. From the business's point of view, it should not be possible to create a timesheet (or timecard) with no Employee Name, or an invalid Employee Name. It should not be possible to create a timesheet for a Project, Task, or Week that doesn't exist. It should not be possible to change the Employee, Project, Task, or Week values in a timesheet after it has been created. It should not be possible to create a timesheet with zero hours. But the table shown above permits all of these things! This illustrates one of the important functions of a data model: it surfaces and documents the business's understanding (and definition) of data, as well as the business rules that constrain data values, so that data cannot be persisted in ways that violate this understanding.

This example also shows why a data model is a valid (and important) application development artifact from the standpoint of Model-Driven Development (MDD). One of the characteristics of an MDD model is that it captures important information about the project that is not captured anywhere else.[9] One statement I often hear from developers is that we don't need data models because data requirements are captured implicitly in the functional user stories (or use cases). However, this obviously is not the case. I'm sure there were user stories that said, "As an Employee Manager, I need to be able to enter and update Employee time cards." But there were clearly no user stories that said, "As a Time Card Record, I need to be a unique instance of an Employee, Project, Task and Week", or "As a Time Card Record, my key attribute values cannot be changed after I've been created." Where are these critical application data requirements captured? In the logical data model!

---

[9] Other characteristics of MDD models: They bring stakeholders together to understand, describe and solve a business problem, they are developed iteratively, as the understanding of the problem grows, they are collectively owned and updated, they are used continually and pervasively both during and after the development process, and they are used to actually generate or implement some aspect of the solution.

However, there is an additional point. Recall that the reason I was sent to this division to fix this problem in the first place was that the project was in certification testing, just prior to a scheduled production deployment, and the application was blowing up every time the testers tried to enter or change a time card record. The project was in grave danger of missing the drop-dead ship date, which is how I became involved. But it raised the question: *Why* was the application failing? It was originally thought that the errors were occurring in the database, but as we've seen, the database allows any sort of data (or no data at all) to be stored in a timesheet record. The problem was obviously occurring in the application. But why?

People who have been application developers (as I have) will probably understand this. When you code an application, you either consciously or unconsciously embed in the code your understanding and assumptions about how things ought to work. The developers who wrote this application had an implicit understanding of how time cards should work and how people should (and should not) be filling them out, and these assumptions were embedded in the code. The testers, on the other hand, were doing what testers always do: trying out hypothetical "edge cases" in the application. "What happens if we enter a time card with no Employee Name?" "What happens if we change the name after creating the time card?" "What happens if we change the Week Number to zero?"

So what we have here are three groups of project stakeholders who are not on the same page about what should and should not be allowed when entering and updating time cards. The developers have hard-coded some assumptions into the application code. The database developers aren't enforcing any data constraints at all, and the testers are doing things the application clearly shouldn't be allowing them to even try! This illustrates another important value aspect of data modeling – it gets everybody on the same page about what the data is, how it is defined, what the permissible values of the data are, what business rules constrain data values, and what integrations of data objects are permissible. In other words, a data model helps everybody keep the story straight!

A data model is intended to tell a story and to bring people together in the creation and telling of the story. The story is about how we will work together to solve a business problem (or seize a business opportunity) using data. The data model becomes, over time, a record of this journey, from inception to eventual success.

LOGICAL VS. PHYSICAL DATA MODELS

At this point, I should note that the statements I've made regarding the value of data modeling really pertain more to logical data models than to physical data models.[10] This will be true of most of what I have to say about data modeling in this book. It's important to make this distinction because most of the arguments I've heard about data modeling no longer being relevant to newer data technologies are really arguments against physical data modeling rather than logical data modeling. For example, Ted Hills, in his excellent book on the COMN modeling language,[11] states that E-R modeling tools cannot represent non-linear datatypes (such as arrays, lists, hierarchies, or composite data types). But this is not true of the logical data model, even in an E-R modeling tool! E-R modeling tools let you define any logical data domain you wish. Here's an example I just created in my E-R tool:

---

[10] There is a lot of confusion regarding the definitions of "logical" vs. "physical" data models, and a lot of people regard these two terms as more-or-less equivalent. In my books, a logical data model expresses the point of view of the business, and is used for communication between business and IT stakeholders. A physical data model (or data design) is a mapping of some subset of the logical data model to an appropriate choice of architecture and technology. In other words, it expresses the physical instantiation of some part of the logical model. A conceptual data model is a (mostly) attribute-free logical data model, used for high-level communication with the business.

[11] Hills, Ted. *NoSQL and SQL Data Modeling* (New Jersey: Technics Publications, 2016).

```
Customer
┌─────────────────────────────────────────┐
│ Customer ID: IDENTIFIER NOT NULL         │
├─────────────────────────────────────────┤
│ Customer Name: NAME NOT NULL             │
│ Customer Address: ADDRESS NOT NULL       │
│ Customer DBA/Alias Name List: LIST NULL  │
│ Customer Order Count By Year: ARRAY NULL │
│ Customer Order History: XML NULL         │
└─────────────────────────────────────────┘
```

In this model, NAME and ADDRESS are complex datatypes, consisting of sub-attributes such as First Name, Last Name, Middle Name, Street Address 1, Street Address 2, City Name, State/Province Code, Postal Code and Country Code.[12]

Not only that, but I can specify a physical instantiation of this logical entity, even in a relational database! Here, for example, is a physical representation of this entity in a table in Microsoft SQL Server:

```
Customer
┌──────────────────────────────────────────────┐
│ CustomerID: integer NOT NULL                 │
├──────────────────────────────────────────────┤
│ CustomerName: udtNameType NOT NULL           │
│ CustomerAddress: udtAddressType NOT NULL     │
│ CustomerDBAAliasNameList: varchar(max) NULL  │
│ CustomerOrderCountByYear: varchar(max) NULL  │
│ CustomerOrderHistory: XML NULL               │
└──────────────────────────────────────────────┘
```

In this table, the complex data attributes CustomerName and CustomerAddress will be implemented as user-defined datatypes (UDTs) in the database. CustomerOrderHistory is no problem since SQL Server provides built-in support for XML documents, even allowing you to combine SQL and XPath in database queries. For the List and Array datatypes, I define them as delimited strings:

```
'First National Bank|First National Bank of Seattle|FirstBank'

'2011|24||2012|28||2013|26||2014|30||2015|32||2016|29'
```

---

[12] This sort of complexity is easier to model using other modeling notations, such as UML and COMN. I'll discuss this in more detail later on. But it's worth noting that you can do this sort of thing even in the more familiar E-R modeling tools.

and then use database functions to parse the strings into table-valued UDTs (this is surprisingly easy to do). Delimited lists are converted into one-dimensional tables, and arrays are converted into two-dimensional tables. References to the functions can be included in the JOIN clause of any SQL query, and the parsed sets returned by the functions are treated exactly like database tables in the join.

Not that this is necessarily how you would want to physically instantiate this data. I understand the limitations of both E-R modeling tools and relational databases. I'm just making the point that these limitations are not as definitive as critics would have you believe.

There are, I believe, three valid criticisms that can be leveled against most E-R modeling tools (Disclaimer: I haven't tried them all). First, they don't always do a good job of logical-to-physical transformation, in cases where the physical structure of the database needs to differ materially from the logical model. Second, E-R modeling tools don't (yet) provide sufficient support for "forward engineering" into non-relational databases.[13] Third, these tools don't adequately support CI/CD (Continuous Integration/Continuous Deployment); it ought to be possible for a CI/CD process to automatically extract and execute the DDL for a database from the data model without human intervention, but it isn't, as of this writing. Hopefully, the tool vendors are working on these problems, and the tools will improve over time.

However, there are ways around some of these limitations. The E-R modeling tool I use has a macro language, and the data model metadata is queryable. This enables me, with some difficulty, to massage the results of the forward-engineering process into customized DDL code that will fit whatever DBMS I

---

[13] A fourth criticism often leveled against E-R modeling tools is that they are not semantically precise. However, I don't believe that effective communication is only about semantics any more than I believe that effective marriages are only about love.

happen to be using.[14] The results of the forward-engineering process can also be exported as XML and massaged using XSLT or similar tools. Data models, themselves, are not accessible to CI/CD processes, but the DDL can easily be extracted and put into a code repository (just like application code) and accessed from there.

The main point I'm trying to make here is that there needs to be a distinction made between logical data modeling, which is easily supported by almost any tool, and physical data design, which may require additional effort to get right. Currently, the process of deriving workable database schema definitions for non-relational databases from E-R modeling tools is harder than it should be, but this does not invalidate the usefulness of logical data modeling per se.[15]

Logical data models are important primarily because they enable different groups of project stakeholders to get together and come to an agreement on the data landscape of the project. This helps everybody have the same understanding about what the data definitions and business rules are. Physical data models are important from the standpoint of Model-Driven Development (MDD): We want to be able to use the data model to iteratively drive the implementation of our logical data model into data structures that can be used by applications and business users. Physical models are also useful in giving IT project stakeholders (including developers, designers, and testers) a common understanding of how the project's data requirements will be physically instantiated.

----

[14] For example, I can use my E-R modeling tool to forward-engineer DDL for Aurora (MySQL) and Snowflake databases in AWS, even though my tool doesn't support these databases natively.

[15] You can also, of course, use a more flexible (non E-R) modeling tool for logical modeling, and then use an E-R modeling tool for physical modeling if you're instantiating into a relational database. Remember, though, that all data models: 1) must tell an understandable data story to all project Stakeholders, and 2) must support an MDD process wherein physical data structures can easily be generated from the data model as it changes.

Key Points

- A data model is not just a description of how data will be instantiated in a database. Data models have higher-valued uses in ensuring that data requirements for a project are properly surfaced and understood, that everybody agrees with data definitions and business rules, and that data cannot be persisted in ways that violate the common understanding of the data requirements.

- Regardless of the technology that will be used to persist data, a data model helps ensure that fundamental questions about data design are asked, discussed, and agreed upon.

- Data models should support the way that people naturally think (and talk) about real-world data objects. They should drive conversations about data meanings and values, surface disagreements about data definitions, inspire discussions about how data could be used to deliver business value, suggest opportunities for the creation of new and potentially useful data objects, and guide intelligent decisions about how data should be captured, stored, used, and integrated.

- A data model is intended to tell a story and to bring people together in the creation and telling of the story. The story is about how we will work together to solve a business problem (or seize a business opportunity) using data. The data model becomes, over time, a record of this journey from inception to eventual success.

- It is important to make a distinction between logical data models, which are used to give business and IT stakeholders a common understanding of business data definitions and rules, and physical data models, which are used to iteratively drive the implementation of some portion of the logical model into some choice of database architecture and technology. Conceptual and logical models are used for communication between business and IT stakeholders, while physical models are used mostly for communication between IT stakeholders. Logical models drive requirements-gathering and specifications, while physical models drive implementation.

Chapter 2
Data Modeling As Storytelling

> *A Theory has only the alternative of being right or wrong. A Model has a third possibility: it may be right, but irrelevant.*
>
> Manfred Eigen

S o, to recap, a data model serves two primary purposes: it helps ensure that data cannot be persisted or used in ways that violate the business' understanding of its business data rules, and it helps get (and keep) everybody on the same page regarding what the data is, how it's defined, how it's persisted, and how it's used.

So now that we know *why* to do data modeling, we can move to the question of *how* to (most effectively) do data modeling. This brings us back to the subject of Model-Driven Development (MDD) mentioned in the previous chapter.

MODEL-DRIVEN DEVELOPMENT

The purpose of MDD is to support the iterative development and deployment of technology solutions. Those solutions are iteratively designed via models (that is, via representations of the solution from different perspectives).

In Model-Driven Development:

- Models are used not just to understand or describe problems, but to implement solutions to them.

- Models are intellectual property, as important as the end product itself.

- Models are used pervasively and continually throughout the development process.

- Models are reused post-implementation to support the solution.

- Models ensure that all project stakeholders understand the work to be done.

The following are the characteristics of an MDD model:

- They capture important information that is not captured elsewhere (as we noted in the previous chapter).

- They describe a limited subset of the problem space (e.g., the data domain of the problem being solved).

- They follow a standard and support design patterns (there are defined standards for data modeling, such as the Rules of Normalization, and there are several books on data model patterns).

- They are unambiguous, clear, and easy-to-understand (if done correctly).

- They can be tested and validated.[16]

---

[16] This is, in my opinion, an aspect of data modeling that has not been sufficiently explored and understood. Very little has been written on this subject, although Steve Hoberman's "Data Model Scorecard®" is a good start (See Steve's book, *Data Modeling Made Simple*, Technics Publications 2005, Chapter 12). Graeme Simsion has proposed a set of acceptance criteria for data models that includes: *completeness, non-redundancy, simplicity and elegance, stability, representation of constraints, reusability* and *comprehensibility*. For my own data models, my

- They are used to generate implementations of the model.

- They are used to support the solution after implementation.

In other words, MDD models serve a two-fold purpose. First, they bring stakeholders together to work out an agreed-upon solution to a problem and to make sure that the solution is understood and agreed to by everyone concerned. Second, the solution itself (or some part of the solution) is generated from the model. As the team's understanding of the problem develops, both the model itself and the generated solution can be iteratively and successively refactored.

So the model becomes the record, the embodiment, if you will, of the story created by the team as it collectively understands and solves a problem.

AGILE MODELS

In addition to supporting MDD, a model should also support an Agile (that is, rapid and iterative) approach to solution development. An Agile model must have the following characteristics:

- It must be created and updated incrementally.

- It must allow the entire team to have input into the development process.

- It must be used to communicate and discuss requirements and lead to shared understanding and agreement.

- It should capture only the necessary amount of information needed to achieve a specific purpose. For data models, this would include the support of conversations needed to drive out, discuss, and come to

---

modeling tool is integrated with a set of canned reports that I use to identify, for example, entities and attributes without business definitions, attributes missing domains, attributes missing classwords, nullable attributes used in unique constraints, etc. This allows me to check the completeness and validity of my data model before it is published.

agreement on data requirements (and their implementation) for a particular sprint, in support of that sprint's goals.

- It must continually move the development effort forward.

- It must deliver maximum value for stakeholder investment.

This assertion that a data model should be both an MDD model and an Agile model gives us insight into how data modeling can be most effectively done. In particular, it tells us that data modeling should be a *group activity* involving at least a representative subset of project stakeholders (including business users, subject-matter experts [SMEs], solution architects, and application analysts). It also tells us that data modeling should be an *iterative* activity, in which the data model is developed as user stories are elaborated, and requirements become more fully understood.

Most importantly, it tells us that a data model is *owned by the team* (that is, the affected stakeholders) and not by the data modeler.[17] Data modelers tend to be extremely proprietary about their models, and this often causes problems on a project. The data modeler tries to impose his/her own will on the model, oftentimes ignoring or overriding the concerns or needs of project stakeholders. The model then becomes an artifact of the modeler's need to create a "perfect" data model (reflecting the modeler's idea of perfection) rather than an artifact of the team's consensus regarding the project's data requirements. The data modeler needs to step back and let the team drive the development of the data model while using his/her expertise to guide and direct the effort and prevent serious mistakes from being made. The resulting data model may not be "perfect" from the modeler's point of view. Still, it will be taken seriously and used by project stakeholders rather than being ignored and disregarded.

---

[17] In simplest terms, logical data models are "owned" by the business, while physical models are "owned" by application support teams.

A data model that is owned by a project team will also be more effective in helping the team understand and think through the important data aspects and issues of a project. As mentioned above, user stories tend to focus exclusively on the functional requirements of a project. Hence, a data model that is embraced by the project team has great value in getting the team to think about the data requirements as well.

A data model needs to be a vehicle for the team to arrive at a shared understanding (and consensus) of the data requirements of the project and of how those requirements will be met. To return to our metaphor, a play that is written by the actors, under the direction of the playwright.[18] This work is vitally necessary to ensure that both the playwright's intention and the expectations of the audience are satisfied.[19]

This approach to data modeling challenges both our notions of what a data model is supposed to be and our understanding of how (and why) data modeling is supposed to be done. In subsequent chapters of this book, we will be exploring this idea more fully, bringing in concepts from storytelling, behavioral psychology, Agile, and Human-Centered Design (HCD).

THE STORY A DATA MODEL TELLS

Every data model tells a story about some aspect of a business or organization. The question that needs to be asked of every data model is: What story is the model telling us, and is it a *true* story? Does the data model tell us a true story

---

[18] What normally happens in the Theatre is that the Playwright delivers the play to the actors and the Director, all of whom hate it. The Playwright then spends several weeks rewriting scenes until everyone is at least resigned, if not happy. This costs a *lot* of money. Then the actors and Director make more changes during rehearsals, usually over the Playwright's strenuous objections. This is the basis for the story about the Playwright who interrupted a rehearsal to say, "Excuse me for interrupting, but I believe I heard a line I wrote!"

[19] As Playwright Jean Kerr put it, "When I go to the Theatre, I like to think that the Playwright has done some work before I got there."

about how the business or organization actually operates?[20] Here's an example: I did a modeling session with the people in our company who write warranty contracts, and we came up with a data model for a new warranty application. When I had a subsequent session with warranty claims adjusters, they told me, "This isn't how warranties work!" We had two separate but closely related departments in the same company working at cross-purposes; it was necessary to bring both groups of people together to discuss and resolve the differences so that the new application would work correctly for everybody.[21]

If you were to look at my company's data models, you would probably be struck by the fact that there is almost never a Customer entity. Why? Because our company sells most of its products through resellers (i.e., Dealers). So you will often see a Dealer entity on our data models, but not a Customer entity. Also, the precise nature of the relationship between a Customer and a Dealer depends upon which of several types of Customer it is and upon which type of Product or Service is being requested. Looking at our data models, you can see clearly the nature of the transaction when, for example, a fleet company leases a group of trucks or an owner-operator needs a replacement truck part or a preventative maintenance service.

As an illustration of how a data model communicates a story about an organization, let's look at a variant of the Employee/Department model we used at the beginning of this book:

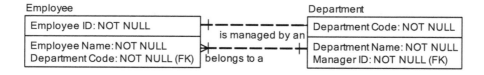

---

[20] We will be exploring this topic in more detail in a subsequent chapter on Business Process Improvement.

[21] We also surfaced a number of business requirements that hadn't been identified in the previous requirements-gathering sessions for the user stories.

This model shows a Many-to-One relationship between Employee and Department, and a One-to-One relationship between Department and Employee (Manager). In other words, it makes the following assertions:

- An Employee can belong to only 1 Department.
- An Employee *must* belong to a Department.
- A Department *must* have at least 1 Employee.
- A Department *must* have a Manager (who is also an Employee).

If you are a data modeler looking at this, you should immediately be challenging these assertions and asking penetrating questions:

- Suppose you wanted to create a new Department for Data Analytics, but hadn't yet received approval or funding for it. You have an opportunity to hire somebody with a proven track record in this type of work. What do you do?

- Suppose you had received approval and funding to create the new Department of Data Analytics, but had not, as yet, hired anyone to staff or manage it. What do you do?

- Suppose the company is downsizing, and you need a Manager to manage more than one Department. What do you do?

- Suppose you want to split an Employee's responsibilities, so as to provide better support for more than one Department. What do you do?

In other words, a good data modeler needs to challenge assertions that are made about the way an organization does business, and make sure the data model accurately reflects how business is being done. The data modeler also needs to make sure the affected stakeholders understand the model's implications and agree on what the model is saying.

In addition to asking whether our data models tell a *true* story, we should also ask whether they tell a *good* story. In other words, our data models should do more than simply document existing business processes; they should spark discussion about how (or whether) those processes should be changed. A data model should lead us to questions like "Is this really what we should be doing?" and "Is there a better way to do this?" In particular, our data model should help us examine whether our current business model is best suited to an emerging or transforming marketplace.[22] Think, for example, about how the emergence of streaming services has impacted the business model of video rental stores. There is no point in doing a data model for an archaic business process or for a business model about to be pushed into obsolescence by emerging technology.

Finally, we must ask whether the data model shows us *a path forward*, from what exists now into what ought to be. Every story ultimately is about a happy ending, a future state that is better than the current *status quo*. Does the data model show us how to get from where we are now to where we want to be (or need to be)? A data model should allow us to explore new ways of using existing data, new ideas for creating or acquiring new data, and new value-creating ways of using data and information technology to create a better future for our organizations.

---

[22] One problem I have with "fact-based modeling" is that it's typically focused on *today's* facts. Such fact-based models don't really capture or support the *evolution* of a company's business processes.

Key Points

- A data model serves three primary purposes. First, it helps ensure that data cannot be persisted or used in ways that violate the business' understanding of its business data rules. Second, it helps get (and keep) everybody on the same page regarding what the data is, how it's defined, how it's persisted, and how it's used. Third, it helps drive discussions about data requirements and surface requirements that may not have been identified in the functional user stories or use cases.

- Data models should be MDD (Model-Driven Development) models. They should enable project stakeholders to collaborate to understand a problem and design and implement its solution.

- Data models should also be Agile models, owned by the affected stakeholders and developed collectively and iteratively.

- Each iteration of the data model should drive the project forward to a successful conclusion and deliver maximum value for the stakeholder's time and effort.

- Data modeling should be a group activity, driven by the project team and directed/guided by the data modeler. The project team should have a collective sense of ownership of the data model. This ensures that the data model will actually be taken seriously and used by the project team.

- Data models should help the project team think through the data-related requirements of the project, as an adjunct to the functional requirements captured in the user stories.

Chapter 3
The Essence of Storytelling

No sentence can be effective if it contains facts alone. It must also contain emotion, image, logic, and promise.

Eugene M. Schwartz

Before we return to the subject of data modeling, I'd like to explore the art of storytelling itself, and introduce some concepts I learned during my time in Toastmasters, the International public-speaking organization.[23] These concepts will be helpful when we return to the discussion of how data modelers can more effectively interact with project stakeholders during modeling sessions.

PRINCIPLES OF STORYTELLING

In storytelling, we often refer to "The Four 'P's": People, Place, Plot, and Purpose.[24] Every story is about some person, in the context of a particular place and time, doing (or trying to do) something to accomplish a particular purpose

---

[23] I served in many capacities in Toastmasters, including Club President and Club Specialist Coordinator.

[24] I would add a fifth "P" – Pace; that is, the tempo of the narrative and story.

or goal. Well guess what? Every project is about a group of people, in the context of a particular business need and technology environment, struggling against all sorts of obstacles to reach a goal or find a solution. In other words, every project is a story that is being told by each of its characters, and it is the individual actions of those characters that determine the outcome of the story! Whether a particular project succeeds or fails is determined, ultimately, by how aware we are of the story and how committed we are to its ending. Every failed project I've been on failed because people either lost sight of what needed to be done or didn't care enough to make it happen.[25]

Every story has three parts: The Setup, The Struggle, and The Solution.[26] The effectiveness of a story depends on how much of the story is dedicated to each of these parts. Here's an illustration from Dave Bailey:

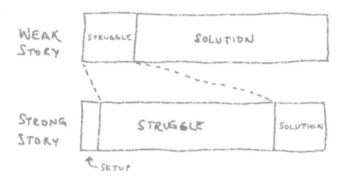

Note that there are two main differences between a weak story and a strong story in this illustration:

- A weak story has no setup, while a strong story does. The setup is the introduction to the story, which brings your audience into the story,

---

[25] It's also fairly common that the delivered solution doesn't actually address the real problem, because the real business issue was never properly identified.

[26] See, for example, Ty Bennet's "The Power of Storytelling" (e-book) at https://bit.ly/3zrBBcl, and Dave Bailey's blog post "12 Storytelling Techniques to Supercharge Your Pitch" at https://bit.ly/3cEV5AQ.

introduces them to the characters and the situation, and explains what is about to happen. The setup is what engages the audience in the story.

- A weak story dwells on the solution (i.e., the "happily ever after" ending) rather than on the struggle. A strong story fully develops and explains the struggle before moving to the solution (ending).

As Dave Bailey puts it, imagine if the first Star Wars movie had started with the destruction of the Death Star!

I mention this because there is a fatal tendency, both in project work and in data modeling, to try to "jump to the ending" too quickly. I've seen project teams try to jump immediately to the first solution that might work instead of taking time to fully understand the problem and ask themselves what sort of solution is and is not appropriate. This is especially true of projects for which a solid application architecture has not been developed and agreed upon at the very beginning. The resulting application becomes a hodge-podge of different technologies that is almost impossible to maintain after deployment.

Similarly, in data modeling, I've seen data modelers try to jump immediately to a modeling solution without allowing the stakeholders to discuss and understand a business problem and surface and resolve conflicts about how the problem should be solved. We, as human beings, tend to want to avoid conflicts or resolve them as quickly as possible and get right to a solution, *any* solution. We need to understand that these conflicts are a necessary part of understanding and solving a business or technology problem, and we need to embrace this process. I can't count the number of times that my initial instincts about solving a data modeling problem turned out to be incorrect once all the facts were on the table.

In other words, the struggle isn't an impediment to the story, the struggle *is* the story!

Here are some of my favorite pieces of advice from Dave Bailey[27]:

- When setting up a story, engage your audience by asking them "You" questions, like "Have *you* ever seen…" or "Do *you* know much about…" or "Hands up if *you* have ever…" (great for groups!).

- Bring your audience into the story by placing them in the scene (again, using "you" statements). For instance, I do a standup comedy bit about surveillance technology in stores; I start the bit by saying, "Take a picture of this: You're pushing your shopping cart around at the hardware store or the local grocery, going from aisle to aisle, taking items off the shelves, looking at them, maybe putting them in your cart, maybe putting them back on the shelf…" This puts the audience in the store with me, where I can start talking about surveillance cameras, sensors, scanners, location trackers, AI, etc.

- Make the characters relatable and the problem familiar. Find ways to connect the audience to the characters and/or situations in your story by relating them to characters and situations they might already be familiar with.

- Stay in the present tense, keep using "You" words instead of "I" words, and use specific details rather than general statements to keep the story real and engaging for your audience.

- Prompt the audience to feel. Our stories are about real-life situations, not just abstract theories. So ask your audience, "How would you feel if…" or "Imagine how it feels when…" questions to connect them with the real-life issues involved in the story.

- Let someone else be the hero. Don't imagine that you have to be the hero of the story. Find ways to give credit to others for their

---

[27] Dave Bailey is a former venture Capitalist who now coaches tech CEOs trying to launch their own startups.

contribution to the solution. Remember, the story is about the solution, not the hero.

LESSONS FROM TOASTMASTERS

One of the most valuable experiences in my life (and one of the best career moves I've ever made) was joining my company's Toastmasters club. It wasn't that I was illiterate or couldn't talk; I couldn't engage effectively with people, especially with groups of people. Imagine being a data modeler who couldn't lead a group discussion! My first speech in Toastmasters was what they call an "ice breaker", a 3-minute introduction of myself and some of my personal interests. I had to read my "ice breaker" speech off a typed page! Now, I travel around the country and give presentations of up to four hours to large groups of people without using any notes. Quite a difference!

Here are some of the lessons I've learned from my experience in Toastmasters that I've tried to apply to my database and data management work:

1) The most important thing to remember is that it's not about *you*, the speaker, teacher, or leader. It's about *them*, your audience or project team, and what they need to hear or know to be successful at what they need or want to do. When you stop to think about it, this is the essence of Agile. An Agile team is a group of people working together to help each other be successful so that the team, as a whole, can reach its goal. The end goal of storytelling is not the telling of the story, it's the impact of the story in the hearts of the audience.

2) Your interactions with people should leave them with something of practical value, something they can take and apply to their lives or work. In Toastmasters, this is called the "takeaway". The point of each speech or story is what each member of the audience will take away from it.

3) Speak to an audience at their level of understanding, using terms and concepts familiar to them. For example, if I'm speaking to application developers about the Rules of Normalization, I'll try to explain it in terms of the object-oriented concepts of cohesion and coupling. Developers won't care if a database is in third normal form, but they will care if an ineffective database design causes cohesion and coupling problems for their application!

4) That being said, always speak from your own knowledge and experience. Tell your own story, not someone else's.

5) Words oftentimes aren't enough to get the point across. You have to find different ways of communicating (e.g., pictures or illustrations, body movements and facial expressions, analogies and metaphors, different tones of voice or mood).

6) You have to quickly adapt how you communicate in response to changing situations (for example, when someone doesn't understand, or disagrees, or gets angry or frustrated). Don't just "plow ahead"; figure out what's happening and adjust your communication accordingly. Always be aware of how your audience is responding to you (or failing to) and have a plan for how to reconnect with them.

7) First impressions are vitally important! Once you lose an audience, it's almost impossible to win them back.

8) You have to capture people's attention quickly (within the first 30 seconds); engage them with a personal reference – a joke, story, or factoid, and let them know right up front how this interaction is likely to be of benefit to them. Give the audience a reason to connect to you and your story.

9) Keep the audience engaged by asking questions, like "Have you ever been in a situation like this?" or "How would you handle this?"

10) It's very important to know what you're talking about and to be factually correct. If your audience starts to think you don't know your subject or are telling them something that isn't true, you've lost them.

11) There's no substitute for enthusiasm. People need to know that you care deeply about what you're talking about. Focus on not just giving people facts, but on sparking their enthusiasm for the subject being discussed.

12) Be concrete (i.e., give practical advice and solutions) and be positive (i.e., dwell on what can be done, not what's impossible). Make sure to give people at least one practical thing they can start doing right away to continue their interest in your subject.

13) Focus on empowering others. Don't try to control the solution to every problem, but teach people how to solve their own problems in whatever way works best for them.

14) Know your audience. Understand what problems they are trying to solve and what their needs are, and speak to those things. I learned early on in my career that people aren't interested in your problems; they're concerned about their own.

15) Be inclusive. Understand the importance of word meanings, slang, gestures, metaphors, body language, eye contact, and personal space pertaining to people of different cultures and backgrounds. Learn what is most important and valued in other cultures. We live and work in an increasingly diverse world, and telling stories in a bubble simply doesn't work.

16) Never stop learning and growing; continually try to find new ways of doing things and adapt your thinking and practice to changes in technology, society, and organizational methodology. The world moves on, and we have to learn to move with it.

17) Don't resist change. Understand it, adapt to it as needed and, if possible, try to anticipate it. For example, during the Covid-19 pandemic, Toastmasters used virtual meetings and online videos to continue its mission.

Most importantly, understand that there is no one "right way" to give a speech or tell a story. Toastmasters teaches lots of useful techniques for improving people's speaking abilities,[28] but in the end, public speaking is about connecting with an audience, holding their attention, and making them feel that the time they have spent with you was valuable. You can't really teach that—you have to do it. Everybody has to figure out what approach(es) work best for them.

That being said, there are many useful skills you can learn that will improve your chances of communicating effectively with any given audience. I would wholeheartedly recommend Toastmasters to any data professional looking to improve his or her communication skills. Go to www.toastmasters.org to find resources and Toastmasters clubs near you.

---

[28] Important note: Toastmasters isn't just about public speaking; they also teach valuable listening, evaluation, critical thinking, team-building and leadership skills.

Key Points

- It is important for data professionals to learn how to communicate effectively with diverse audiences. Effective communication is the foundation for success in our profession.

- Understand your audience and focus on their needs and concerns. What is their level of knowledge and interest in your subject? What do they need to understand, learn or discover? How can you best help them succeed?

- Make sure your audience has at least one practical "takeaway", something they can start using right away to achieve success.

- Speak to people on their level, using language and analogies that are familiar to them. Don't speak over people, and don't assume they're not capable of understanding what you're saying. Make sure to stay connected to your audience throughout your presentation.

- Speak from your own personal knowledge and experience. Tell your own story, not someone else's.

- Be inclusive, and understand how things like word meanings, slang, overuse of acronyms, gestures, metaphors, body language, eye contact, and personal space affect how you can effectively communicate with people of other cultures.

- Focus on empowering people to find ways of solving their own problems. Don't try to solve everybody's problems for them or insist on solving every problem a certain way.

- Don't resist change. Our profession is a lifelong process of learning new skills, adapting to changing technologies and ways of doing things, and finding new ways of applying data management principles in ever-evolving arenas of endeavor.

- There is no single "right way" of communicating with a given audience. Learn the basic skills and rely on intelligence guided by experience to direct your interactions.

Chapter 4
Who Is Our Audience?

All stakeholders must participate in the gains and losses of any particular situation.

Christine Lagarde

Now that we've thought about how best to tell our story, let's consider the people we're telling it to. As I said before, it's important to understand your audience and to gauge how much they know (or care) about your subject before you start talking. The storyteller needs to find ways of engaging the audience at the very beginning and draw them into the story.

If you're a data professional, you will be interacting with many different types of people, each having different needs, different points of view, and different levels of understanding about data issues. You will have to find ways of engaging with each of these groups, eliciting their concerns and needs, and demonstrating ways that you can help them achieve the success they seek.

THE IMPORTANCE OF STAKEHOLDERS

I've always written about data work from a stakeholder perspective. In business terms, a stakeholder is a person or group that has *any* sort of interest in the success or failure of a given initiative. It may be a person or group with a vested interest in seeing the initiative succeed, or it may be a person or group with a vested interest in seeing the initiative fail. In either case, we need to be aware of their interest and take appropriate action to enable the people who can help us succeed and forestall the people who might cause us to fail. As I explained in my first book,[29] a business has many different groups of stakeholders (including customers, vendors, dealers, employees, and shareholders). Even competitors and regulators should be considered stakeholders. Engaged in the right way, a competitor can become an ally; handled in the wrong way, a regulator can become an implacable (and expensive) enemy.[30]

Stakeholder management is the key to success, both in business and in every other field of human endeavor. Companies that don't treat their employees right won't have skilled (and dedicated) labor. Companies that don't treat their resellers right won't see increased market share. Companies that don't treat their shareholders right won't have needed capital for growth and expansion. Companies that don't treat their vendors right won't get quality parts at a fair price, timely deliveries, or good service. Companies that don't treat regulators right will see endless (and expensive) litigation. Conversely, stakeholders that are treated fairly will become allies in the company's success. As I've often said,

---

[29] Building the Agile Database, Chapter 1.

[30] As a great poet (me) once wrote:
> *In every foreign nation,*
> *On every city street,*
> *There's an ally and an enemy*
> *In everyone you meet.*

you will be successful only to the extent that you can convince others to want you to succeed.

Data professionals need to heed this warning: There are too many people, both in business and in IT, who would rather fry eggs on their fingernails than listen to a data modeler drone on about normalization and standards and semantics and ontologies and the best sort of notation to use, all while ignoring the actual concerns of business and IT stakeholders who are trying to successfully complete a project or deploy an application. As I said before, the story isn't about us or what we need—it's about our audience and what they need. We will be successful only insofar as we can make them successful; if we do not help them succeed, they will help us fail.

TYPES OF DATA MANAGEMENT STAKEHOLDERS

So what are the stakeholder groups that we, as data professionals, need to interact with, and how can we respond effectively to their needs? Here is a list (not comprehensive or complete[31]) of the people we most often work with on projects, the kinds of stories they prefer to tell, and how we can help them tell their stories:

- Business people are most comfortable with *process* stories (that is, stories about *how* a process is being done or ought to be done). Business users want to know what data entities and attributes are associated with a particular business process. For this group, a data flow diagram (DFD) is often helpful in showing the association between business processes and data entities. DFDs are also useful for exploring and asking questions about whether or how a business process can be changed or made more efficient.

---

[31] There is a more comprehensive list of project Stakeholders in Chapter 1 of my book, *Building the Agile Database* (pp. 30-32).

- IT people (such as application developers) are most comfortable with *functional* stories (that is, stories about *what* needs to be done and why). Developers want to be sure that the data structures we model and implement adequately support their object classes, methods, and APIs. For this group, a UML Activity or Sequence diagram is useful for showing the flow of functional activities associated with the users of an application. These diagrams also surface entities that will be needed in the data model. From these diagrams, a UML class diagram is created, showing the object classes, their data properties, and their associated methods. The properties portion of a UML class diagram is roughly equivalent to a conceptual data model.[32]

- Data analysts are usually concerned with *business rules* stories (that is, the rules or semantic definitions that constrain the values of data). They want to know that reporting and analytics based on application data will make sense to line-of-business users and will be correct enough to base business decision-making upon. A logical data model is the best fit for these requirements. I usually extract metadata from the data model into either a Word document (suitably formatted) or an Excel spreadsheet to make the metadata more easily understood by business users.

- Project managers deal in *historical narratives* ("Here's where we started from, here's how we got to where we are now, and here's what we need to do to get to where we want to be"). From a data perspective, what project managers are most interested in is the association between data entities and user stories; for example, "How many entities do we need to model and deploy to support these ten user

---

[32] For an explanation, and examples, of UML diagrams used by application developers, please see Chapter 2 of Scott Ambler's book, *Agile Database Techniques* (Wiley Publishing, 2003). Another good UML reference is Martin Fowler's *UML Distilled* (Addison Wesley Longman, Inc, 1997).

stories?" I will often argue to project managers that a certain set of entities should be modeled because they are need to support common user stories in upcoming sprints.[33] It is a good idea, on Agile projects, for a data modeler to capture the associations of entities and attributes to user stories; this way, when user stories are dropped or changed, we will know what changes need to be made to the data model. I use user-defined properties (UDPs) in my data model to capture the associations between entities/attributes and user stories. Then I print out and report this metadata to the project manager, showing how an entity impacts/supports the user stories.

- Quality Assurance (QA) analysts and testers are more concerned with *individual battle* stories than an overall war documentary. They want to ensure that the software being developed satisfies user requirements and provides a positive user experience. To this end, they develop and execute test cases based on the acceptance criteria of each user story. With QA people, I've found that it's very useful for them to understand the data model (especially the physical model), the primary key, alternate key(s), and other data attribute constraints, and the (foreign key) relationships between tables. This metadata can also be extracted from the data model into report form for easier consumption. QA people will also benefit from the sort of report described above, showing the association of entities and attributes (or, in this context, tables, and columns) with user stories. This helps them be aware of what data to check for in the database after the execution of each test, and what sort of errors might occur in the database during testing.

---

[33] In *Building the Agile Database*, I argue that it's OK, at least to some extent, to model in advance of the user stories, since the effort involved in refactoring data models is minimal, and the models can be used to guide discussions about the user stories. However, we should only *implement* what is needed to support user story development.

- Management prefers tales of epic accomplishments, such as, "This is what we have been able to accomplish, against all odds." What management wants to hear is that everybody is doing what is necessary to make the project a success. What management does *not* want to hear is that the project will be delayed for three weeks because the project team can't agree on the data model or the database design. *Always* make sure that the story you tell management is the story of how your contributions are enabling higher-quality work to be done more quickly!

In other words, data professionals need to understand what sort of story is being told by each group of project stakeholders, and they need to know how best to help them tell that story. At the same time, we data professionals need to know what sort of story we need to tell, and we need to know how to get the help we need from the other stakeholders to tell it. The story we want to tell together is how the project was a success, and our end customers were made happy and more productive. So, whatever we, as data professionals, can do to help our project stakeholders and team members be successful (while still adhering to good data management practices) is important and worthwhile work.

COMMUNICATING WITH STAKEHOLDERS

As indicated above, each group of project stakeholders will see the project from a different point of view. Each has different arenas of expertise, different areas of concern, and different requirements. The definition of "success" is different for each group, and we need to understand what "success" means to each of them. When communicating with stakeholders, we need to keep in mind the following questions:

- What knowledge and experience do they have? What is their point of view?

- What is their interest in this project? What are they hoping to accomplish?

- What are they contributing to this project?

- What do they need to be successful?

- How can I help them to be successful?

- How can I best engage their interest and participation in my data management activities?

- What sort of education or context do they need to understand what I'm trying to do?

The most important rule of communicating with stakeholders is: *Let People Tell Their Story.* Too often, we talk over or around people because we're more interested in what we're trying to accomplish than in what they are trying to accomplish. But if we don't listen to what they're trying to tell us, we will miss important information, make invalid assumptions, and go off in the wrong direction. This will lead, later on, to project defects and expensive rework. We need to redirect our focus to what our stakeholders (our customers) need to successfully obtain their necessary contributions to the success of our project.

At the same time, we also need to communicate clearly to our stakeholders what we, ourselves, need to be successful at what we are trying to do and convince them that helping us succeed will enable us to help them succeed as well. We need to explain – and demonstrate – to our project stakeholders that a well-defined data model will contribute material value to the success of the project:

- It will help everyone on the project understand the business data requirements of the project and the business rules that the data needs to adhere to.

- It will assist the project team when discussing requirements, elaborating user stories, and discussing application architecture and design.

- It will expedite the work of designing, creating, and refactoring database structures and other database objects.

- It will also expedite migrating data from legacy systems into the new application's data structures and identifying potential data quality issues ahead of time.

- It will help the QA team create, execute, and evaluate test cases for the application.

- It will assist business analysts who will want to do reporting and analytics on the application data after it's created.

- It will assist DBAs and application support people who will need to maintain and troubleshoot the application and database after production deployment.

- It will facilitate the reuse of this data in support of other projects and business initiatives.

A TRUE STORY

For stakeholders who are not convinced of the value of a well-defined data model and database design, I like to relate a story that was told to me by my good friend and colleague John Giles[34].

---

[34] John is the author of *The Nimble Elephant* (Technics Publications, 2012) and *The Elephant in the Fridge* (Technics Publications, 2019). John is a very skilled Data practitioner, data vault expert, and a heck of a great guy. You will get to hear some of his stories in this book. John credits the School Records story to Graham Witt, an Australia-based data modeler.

A school district created a student records database for its schools, but designed it with only a single set of address-related fields for each student (operating on the assumption that the parent or parents of each child lived at the same address as the child). They failed to consider that, in cases of divorce or separation, the parents might be living apart. They also failed to consider that, in cases of abuse, one parent might not want the other parent to know where they were living.

This faulty assumption enabled one man, a domestic abuser, to find the shelter where his estranged wife and child were staying.

This is the sort of concern that a skilled data practitioner could have surfaced early on during data modeling, and probably forestalled by asking the right sort of questions and by identifying (and challenging) assumptions. This is an example of the sort of value a skilled data practitioner can bring to a project.

The principal responsibility of a data practitioner is to *make sure the data story is told right*! And also to make sure the data story is *understood* by the other project stakeholders.

Key Points

- We need to understand the needs and concerns of all stakeholders associated with a project and be able to help them succeed at what they need to do to ensure that the project, as a whole, is a success.

- We also need to understand what story each stakeholder group wants to tell and assist them in telling that story. These stories surface important project requirements, including data and process requirements that we need to understand to do our jobs effectively.

- We should master different ways of communicating effectively with each stakeholder group, using whatever tools, techniques, and models each group is comfortable using, whether it's a report, a spreadsheet, a Data Flow Diagram, or a UML Class Model.

- We also need to tell our own story, the story of the value we are contributing to the project, and what we need from our stakeholders to do our work successfully.

- We need to let people tell their own story in their own way, rather than talking over them or around them and focusing on our own concerns. People need to feel that their concerns are understood and that their input is appreciated. This will give them a sense of ownership of the final product (e.g., the data model) and will make them more willing to use it and appreciate its value.

- The principal responsibility of a Data practitioner is to *make sure the data story is told right* and also to make sure the data story is understood by the other project stakeholders.

Chapter 5
Data Model Shamanism

Looking behind, I am filled with gratitude; looking forward, I am filled with vision; looking upwards, I am filled with strength; looking within, I discover peace.

Quero Apache Prayer

Let's go back to the image we introduced at the beginning of this book. Imagine yourself seated around a campfire late at night, surrounded by members of your tribe. An elder rises and takes his place at the front of the group. He is the Shaman, the tribe's historian and storyteller. He recounts the stories of the origin of the tribe, of its journeys across the land to its present home, its trials and victories, its dreams and aspirations and values. As he speaks, his words bring the tribe together in a common sense of purpose. Tomorrow will be a difficult day, a day filled with challenge and hardship. All must work together and sacrifice their own comfort for the common good. The words and stories of the Shaman will sustain the tribe in its efforts until success is achieved.

SHAMANISM EXPLAINED

The word "Shaman" literally means "one who knows"; in other words, Shamans are the "knowledge managers" of the tribe. They are the custodians of the tribe's store of knowledge, wisdom, and expertise, and can take on several different roles within the tribe[35]:

- *Communicator*: The ability to provide help and advice to members of the tribe.

- *Educator*: The keeper of myth, tradition, and tribal wisdom.

- *Healer*: Helping to treat sickness and address/solve problems within the tribe.

- *Prophet*: Helping the tribe anticipate and prepare for future opportunities.

The Shaman:

- Documents the history of what has been done in the past and helps the tribe understand how they got to where they are now.

- Preserves a culture that unifies and sustains the tribe.

- Teaches life lessons, such as the importance of honor and truthfulness.

- Suggests strategies (through storytelling and prophecy) to help the tribe solve problems or accomplish a goal.

- Emphasizes the connections between the tribe and the world around them (i.e., symbiosis).

---

[35] See, for example, the definition of "Shaman" found at https://bit.ly/3xoYHPp.

- Helps provide stability, unity, and cohesion in times of crisis (such as the forced relocation of the tribe).

Moreover, lest you think that Shamans act only in an advisory capacity, understand that Shamans also have a facilitator or implementer role in the tribe. In some tribes, such as the Cheyenne and the Sioux, the Shaman was also the War Chief, leading the tribe into battle!

SHAMANISM IN DATA MANAGEMENT

So what does all this have to do with data management, you may ask? The inference is obvious: data managers take on several Shaman-like roles within an organization. They are the custodians of knowledge about an organization's data assets. They understand what has been done with data in the past and can help chart new opportunities for leveraging those data assets in the future. They work with business users and IT to develop new data and BI technologies that increase an organization's store of knowledge and ability to deliver value to stakeholders. They work to keep an organization's store of knowledge current, correct, and easy to consume. They help understand and solve data- and knowledge-related problems within an organization. They help guide an organization through challenging times and changing business conditions, and they provide insight as to appropriate and inappropriate ways of using data to achieve business goals.

Most importantly, they can tell the story of the importance of data management and the value that good data practices can contribute to an organization. Conversely, they can also tell stories about the consequences of bad data practices, such as the one at the end of the last chapter. As I said in *Building the Agile Database*, even our project failures have value because we can always point to them as examples of what *not* to do next time.[36]

---

[36] There is an excellent book by Scott Taylor called *Telling Your Data Story* (Technics Publications, 2020) that explains how data professionals can better tell their data stories.

Let's focus, for the moment, on the role of data modeling within an organization. Data modelers are commonly regarded as nothing more than documenters or implementers of data requirements. If I had a dollar for every request I've received along the lines of "Please create the following table" or "Please add the following column to Table A", I'd be sunning on my yacht in the Caribbean! But this is not the real work of data modeling. Data modelers have to understand both the context of the data environment pertaining to the request and the real business reason for the request. Does the request fit meaningfully into the context of the data? Does the request help meet a legitimate business need or accomplish a legitimate business goal? Will implementing the request improve the data environment and make it better able to meet the organization's needs?

In many instances, I've had to push back on such requests as either not necessary, already implemented elsewhere, not appropriate, or needing to be implemented differently. In my first book, I recount the story of how insufficient attention to a request for a data model and database change led to significant problems for an application (and its associated business process).[37] Inappropriately denormalizing several supertype/subtype relationships in the database led to greatly increased stored procedure complexity and greatly reduced performance!

Data modelers need more than just data modeling skills. They also need facilitation and communication skills, including the ability to manage conversations around data requirements, ask pertinent questions, surface assumptions, and push back (as necessary) when requests don't seem to make sense, or could be implemented in a more appropriate way. They need to make sure that everybody is telling (and hearing) the same story, that requests for data model and database changes facilitate the work that everybody agrees needs to be done, and that these requests move the organization's data, information, and knowledge management capabilities forward.

---

[37] Burns, Larry. *Building the Agile Database* (Technics Publications, 2011), pp. 148-150.

In the same way that members of a tribe wouldn't ask the Shaman to cast a particular spell or utter a particular prophecy, we need to understand that data management professionals need to be regarded as facilitators and problem-solvers, as people whose role is to understand current and future business needs and opportunities in the context of an organization's current data and information assets. Their job is to help chart and direct the future development of those assets, with an eye toward increasing the delivery of knowledge and value.

THE SHAMAN AS TRIBAL HISTORIAN

One of the Shaman's most important assets is his/her ability to bring the knowledge of the past to bear on the problems of today. When solving problems, it's important not to "reinvent the wheel" when it's just a spoke that needs replacing. This is especially true on Agile projects, with their notoriously tight cycle times.

The Shaman is the keeper of a comprehensive encyclopedia of the tribe – its history, its religion, medicines, spells, chants, prayers, and music. The Shaman can draw on all of this past knowledge and experience to address the current needs of the tribe.

In the same way, the data modeler does not develop data models from scratch; he or she must draw from at least two sources of past knowledge:

- Existing data models related to the business area under discussion, especially enterprise or canonical data models (if any exist). Whenever I'm starting a data model, or building a database, I always ask, "Is this something that has been modeled before? Has it been implemented anywhere else? Does this data model, database, or data currently exist (in any form) anywhere else in the organization? If so, where?"

- Universal data model patterns (ala David Hay, Len Silverston, etc.). Data model patterns provide insight into how business data problems have been solved in the past. In Chapter 18, I provide an example of how I used data model patterns to solve a difficult database design problem for an important project. And in Chapter 6, I discuss using data model patterns to "jump start" data modeling discussions and data requirements analysis. John Giles quotes Len Silverston as stating that 50% or more of an organization's enterprise data requirements are covered by these common, industry-neutral patterns.[38] John's book *The Nimble Elephant* provides many examples of how to effectively use data model patterns for both Agile projects and enterprise data modeling.

As with Shamans, data professionals need to understand how to apply the knowledge of the past to solve the problems of today.

---

[38] Giles, John. *The Nimble Elephant* (New Jersey: Technics Publications LLC, 2012), p. 15.

Key Points

- Shamans are the "knowledge managers" of the tribe. They are the custodians of the tribe's store of knowledge, wisdom, and expertise, and can take on the roles of Communicator, Educator, Healer, and Prophet.

- Shamans are historians, teachers, problem solvers, facilitators, and implementers. They help the tribe understand what has been done in the past and guide their actions in the present.

- Data Managers take on several Shaman-like roles within an organization. They are the custodians of knowledge about an organization's data assets. They understand what has been done with data in the past and can help chart new opportunities for leveraging those data assets in the future.

- Data Managers can tell the story of the importance of data management and the value that good Data practices can contribute to an organization. Conversely, they can also tell stories about the consequences of bad Data practices and the need to avoid them.

- Data modelers are not just documenters or implementers of data requirements. Data modelers have to understand the context of the data environment about the request and the real business reason for the request.

- Data modelers need communication and facilitation skills to ensure that everybody is telling (and hearing) the same story, that requests for data model and database changes facilitate the work that everybody agrees needs to be done, and that these requests move the organization's data, information, and knowledge management capabilities forward.

- Data modelers can use existing data models and data model patterns to "jump start" the development of data models for current projects.

Chapter 6
Interactive Data Modeling

What is explained can be denied, but what is felt cannot be forgotten.

Charles Bowden

So how do we take a "Shamanistic" approach to data modeling, and at the same time make it more Agile? First and foremost, we need to make data modeling a more interactive activity! No more of this "Give me the requirements, and I'll get back to you with a data model in two or three weeks." Agile is an interactive process in which stakeholders collaborate together on a problem in order to find a solution. Therefore, the first responsibility of a data modeler is to get all affected stakeholders involved in creating the data model.

APPROACHES TO INTERACTIVE MODELING

There are several different ways to do this, and no one method will work for all projects. The data modeler needs to find the particular method of interaction that will work with a particular project team. If one method isn't working, abandon it quickly and try another (this is the approach used in Human-Centered Design). Any given approach will be successful only insofar as it: a) engages the interests of the stakeholders involved and b) continually surfaces important information about the data requirements of the project. Here are some of the techniques I've used in past projects:

- A "sticky note" (or "flash card") approach is often effective, especially when you can get your stakeholders organized into small teams to collaborate on the identification of entities, attributes, and relationships.[39] Each small team puts its contributions up on the board, and then everything is reviewed by the entire group. I use special, color-coded blank stickies (or cards) for entities, attributes, and relationships that explain what information we are trying to collect for the data model. Figure 1 (on page 77) shows the cards I use for Entity/ Relationship/Attribute (ERA) modeling. I also have a similar set of cards for Object-Role modeling (see Figure 2 on page 78), although I don't use this method as much.

  This method is more effective with stakeholders who have some understanding of data and its specification. I always spend some time at the beginning of the modeling session explaining basic data concepts. In some cases, you may need to simplify some of the items on the cards and cover different items in different sessions. Do whatever you have to make this process as easy – and fun – as possible for the participants. Let them choose what parts of the model to work on at any given time and have rewards handy (like a big bowl of chocolates) for, say, the participant who identifies the most entities or attributes!

- Since most business users work extensively with spreadsheets, these can be an effective modeling tool, even for non-relational databases (business users are quite accustomed to creating hierarchies on

---

[39] A similar sort of approach is used in UML, called "CRC Cards". These cards identify object *Classes*, denote the *Responsibilities* (methods) associated with each class, and then identify the *Collaborators* (data entity or entities) that support each method. See pp. 64-65 of Martin Fowler's book *UML Distilled*.

spreadsheets). Start with the business spreadsheets that are already being used to capture, analyze and report data, and break them out into entities, attributes, and relationships.

For new applications (for which the data doesn't currently exist), have the business users create spreadsheets of how they think the data will look (or ought to look), and how it will be reported to management. Then walk through the spreadsheets and ask questions to surface additional information and potential problems. Although this technique is most effective with business users, I've found that many, if not most, application developers are also comfortable with this approach.

- One very effective technique is to have participants just "draw" the data on the whiteboard. These whiteboard drawings tend to look very much like spreadsheets (relational) or documents (hierarchical). Afterward, the group can ask questions to surface additional information about the data. This approach tends to be most effective with application development teams, who are used to "whiteboarding" solutions to problems.

- As mentioned previously, with a business audience, you could start with a high-level Data Flow Diagram (DFD) showing the relationship between business processes and data objects. With an audience of application developers, you could start with a UML activity or sequence diagram (showing the relationship between data entities and user or process activities), or a UML class model (whose object classes and properties can be mapped to logical entities and attributes).

- For process modeling or DFDs, another useful technique is *storyboarding*. In storyboarding, participants create a series of cartoon-like panels that explain a process in step-by-step detail. These panels can then be linked to the appropriate data stores.

- The best way to speed up the modeling process (especially with a novice audience) is to start with a "straw man" data model for people to look at and critique. My good friend and colleague, John Giles, likes to start by presenting his audience with a universal data model pattern (from someone like David Hay or Len Silverston), that is relevant to the current business need or problem. The ensuing discussion surfaces useful information about where and how the current business problem or its context differs from the pattern. The modeler can also create a draft data model to use as a jumping-off point for the discussion, making use of any existing data models that cover the same business data entities (such as Customer or Product).

- I've also done interactive modeling using my data modeling tool of choice. I project a blank data model (template) on a screen and then ask questions to get people started talking about the data. If someone mentions, for example, an entity, I create it on the model, we label it, and then talk about its business definition and other characteristics. Similarly, if someone mentions an attribute or a relationship, I put it on the model, we discuss it, and I capture the necessary information in the model.

One advantage of using a modeling tool is that I can use User-Defined Properties (UDPs) in my modeling template to allow me to capture the information I need about each entity, attribute and relationship, right at the moment we're discussing it. I can also capture notes about the discussion itself, including assumptions made or differences of opinion about how something should be named and defined. And I don't need to rely on my notes or my memory! Another advantage is that I don't have to spend time transferring information captured on sticky notes, documents, or spreadsheets into the data model—

oftentimes, I can click a button and generate the next version of the database on the spot!

The disadvantage of this approach is that it doesn't work well unless the participants are conversant with data models and the basic process and purpose of data modeling. You may have to explain how data modeling works as you're going along and what it is you're trying to accomplish with the data model, so that people won't regard it as just unnecessary documentation.

Not all of these approaches work or work equally well, for any given audience. The modeler will have to "feel out" each individual audience and rely on some trial-and-error to find the best approach. The important thing is to ensure that the audience feels a sense of contribution and ownership of the data model, and believe that it accurately reflects their understanding of the business.

OTHER TYPES OF INTERACTION

The practice of Human-Centered Design, or HCD, which we will be talking about later in this book, has sparked the development of several different ways of communicating among stakeholders, brainstorming ideas, and visualizing the results.[40] Some of these concepts include:

- *Frameworks*. A Framework is a visual representation of a system, showing the critical relationships between concepts or sets of ideas. The graphical Table of Contents at the beginning of this book is an example of a Framework. Types of Frameworks include:

    o *Journey Maps*: Journey Maps allow you to visualize a process from beginning to end, and to see the entire flow of a user experience.

---

[40] See, for example, *The Field Guide to Human-Centered Design* (IDEO.org, 2015).

Data Flow Diagrams (DFDs) and UML activity diagrams are examples of journey maps.

o *Relational Maps*: Relational maps are used to visualize how different ideas relate to one another (like our graphical table of contents). "Mind maps" are examples of relational maps.

o *Axis Maps*: Axis maps use sets of X-Y (or X-Y-Z) coordinates on a graph to show patterns and relationships between ideas. For example, you could plot the results of a survey showing people's responses to new technology. The X-axis could show risk-taking vs. risk-averse behavior; the Y-axis could show a range of technology options (say, cloud-based to server-based); and the Z-axis could show the availability of technology enablers (say, access to high-speed Internet) in the respondent's area.

- *Brainstorming*. Brainstorming brings a group of people together to "crowd source" a solution to a problem. The focus is on generating as many new ideas as possible—the actual evaluation and discussion of the ideas comes later. Ideas are captured using sticky notes or a whiteboard, and the rule is to defer judgment and encourage creative, "out of the box" thinking. An initial question of the form, "How might we…?" or "I wish…" is used to start the ball rolling. After the brainstorming session, you can ask the attendees to select their "Top Five" ideas that really captured their interest and imagination.

- *Card Sort*. One way to evaluate end-user support for a set of options is to give them a set of cards that depict those options and ask them to sort the cards in order of importance (to the end-user). This shows us what things are most important to the largest number of people. For example, a company that was trying to market solar-powered lamps in rural communities gave people a set of cards with pictures of animals on them, and asked them to select which animals most closely represented solar-power to them.[41] Most of the people selected pictures of cows and chickens, showing that they considered solar power to be a potentially valuable asset. Had they selected pictures of, say, eagles or snakes, the company would have concluded there was much less potential support for their product.

- *Collage.* In collage, participants in a focus group or other similar team endeavor use art materials (paper, cardboard, tape, markers, etc.) to construct a visual model of a proposed solution to a problem. This isn't a working model, of course; it's simply a visualization of how people think a solution will work (or ought to work). For example, end-users could use collaging to show how they would like the user interface of a proposed new application to work. You could, theoretically, even use collaging to create a high-level, user-driven conceptual data model (or DFD)!

Data modeling is, let's face it, an extremely boring and tedious exercise for most people (especially business users). Anything we can do to pique their interest, capture their attention, and unlock their imaginations is well worth our consideration!

ADVANTAGES TO INTERACTIVE MODELING

The important thing, as I've said before, is that everybody needs to feel as though their voice has been heard and their contributions noted and appreciated. Everybody needs to feel as though they have a stakeholder interest in the creation of the data model, so that everybody will accept it as the specification of their data requirements. Everybody needs to be on the same page about what the data requirements are and about how they are going to be implemented for the project. The data model should be the driver for conversations about data requirements and their implementation throughout the project. On projects that

---

[41] Ibid, p. 58.

I've worked on, it's been very gratifying to see both developers and business users referencing my data models during discussions and elaborations of user stories and application requirements. Our quality assurance people and testers also use them when creating and executing tests and evaluating the test results. And our application support people reference them when troubleshooting problems with the applications post-production.

MODELS THAT TALK

I think it's very important that a data model communicate as much information as possible, anticipating the questions that might be asked by customers and addressing assumptions that might erroneously be made. First off, I use a system of color-coding in my data models.[42] There is a legend at the top-left of the model with an explanation of the model, version number, and explanation of the color-coding:

Warranty Claim - Applicable Warranties Version 001a - Draft As Of January 25, 2021 Proprietary Information
Modified Entity or Attribute
New Entity or Attribute
Logical-Only Entity or Attribute Physical-Only Entity or Attribute
Delegated Table
Reference Entity

I also keep a log of changes to the model in a text box at the top of the model:

---

[42] This color-coding tends to benefit other members of the data team more than, say, developers, as it isn't always possible to print the models out in color, and PDFs of the models don't always show the coloring of the fonts or the shading.

> Mod. April 10, 2019 LEB per Naveta: Remove Chassis Excluded Option from data model.
> Mod. August 20, 2019 LEB per Ankush: Added Claim Type Code to Coverage Type.
> Mod. 10/20/2020 LEB per Ankush: Added unique constraint on COVERAGE_TYPE_NAME in table PACR_COVERAGE_TYPE.
> Mod. 01/25/2021 LEB, per Lavanya: Added new table to hold output from OTA/SIR API service.

And I use a text box for keeping track of questions raised and items under discussion[43]:

> Question 1: Do we need to support Contract Term Groups in the ODS?
> Question 2: What is the size of Contract Purchasing Group Code?

These text boxes are also useful for specifying complex business rules that may need to be implemented in application code or perhaps a database trigger.

As noted above, new entities and attributes are denoted by red font; changes to entities or attributes are denoted by blue font[44]:

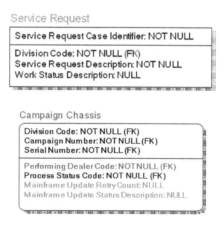

_____

[43] It would also be a good idea to note who asked the question or raised the issue. If the comment is associated with a particular user story, note that as well.

[44] When converting the models to PDFs, make sure that the colorings are captured!

When Attributes are deleted from the model as no longer needed, I will often document this fact by putting a strike-through across the attribute name, and then marking the attribute as logical-only:

When there is a possibility of a question about why something was done a certain way in the model, I will always include a text box with an explanation:

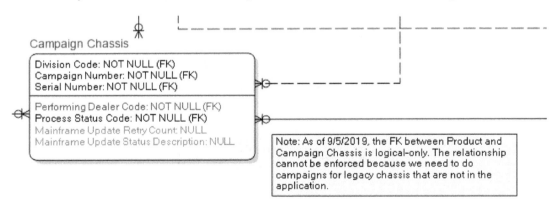

Reference data is denoted by light-blue shading:

Country

| Country Code: NOT NULL |
| Country Name: NOT NULL |

Logical-only entities or attributes (in the logical model), or physical-only tables or columns (in the physical model) are denoted by purple font:

Dealer Service Status

| Dealer Service Status Code: NOT NULL |
| Dealer Service Status Description: NOT NULL |

On my current project, which involves using a commercial, off-the-shelf (COTS) software package, I've had to deal with something I've never previously encountered: the use of customer-maintained application database tables (these are referred to as *delegated tables*). Delegated tables allow application business users to maintain master or reference data on spreadsheets or comma-delimited files, and upload that data directly into the application. Needless to say, this has presented some interesting modeling challenges, as the table definitions need to match corresponding application screens. For this reason, these tables may contain duplicate or redundant data attributes, which can be confusing for people looking at the data model. Here's an example:

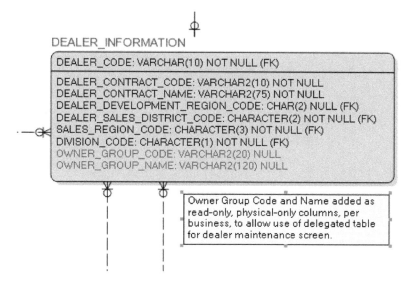

In this case, I've used green shading to denote that this physical entity is a delegated table. I've highlighted two columns that are redundant (they are actually attributes of a different entity in the data model and have been included in the delegated table for the convenience of the business users maintaining the data). These columns are defined in the data model as physical-only. I've also added an explanatory comment.

Also, although I have never done this, you could consider using different types of fonts, or italics or bolding, to indicate new or modified entities and attributes. Just make sure there is a legend at the top of the model to explain what each type of font means.

When I model, I always think about the various stakeholders using, referencing, or updating the model. I try to anticipate their questions, assumptions they may make, confusion they may encounter, and I try to address them in the model so that it provides the maximum amount of value with the least amount of effort.

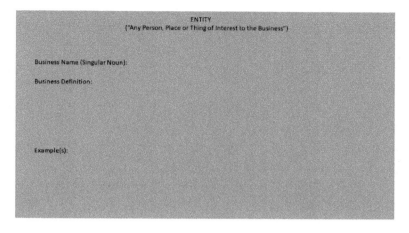

ENTITY
("Any Person, Place or Thing of Interest to the Business")

Business Name (Singular Noun):

Business Definition:

Example(s):

ATTRIBUTE
("A Characteristic or Property of an Entity")

Business Name (Singular Adjective):

Business Definition:

Domain/Class[1]:

Constraints[2]:

Required (Yes/No)?

Key Attribute (Yes/No)?

Example(s):

[1] e.g., Name, Date, Number, Integer, String, List, Text, Object
[2] e.g., Length, Value or Range restrictions

RELATIONSHIP
("An Association Between Two Entities")

Relationship Type[1]:

Parent-to-Child Phrase[2]:

Child-to-Parent Phrase[2]:

Required (Yes/No)?

Cardinality[3]:

Business Rule(s):

[1] e.g., Association, Aggregation, Composition, Subtype
[2] Usually one or the other, not both
[3] Zero or One Parent to Zero, 1, N or M(any) Children

Figure 1: Flash Cards for ERA Modeling.

ENTITY TYPE
("Anything We Can Assert a Fact About")

Entity Type Name (Singular Noun):

Reference Mode[1]:

Definition:

Domain/Class[2]:

Example(s):

[1]The manner in which we refer to a single instance of the entity type; e.g. "Name", "Number", or "ID"
[2]e.g., Name, Date, Number, Integer, String, List, Text, Object

FACT TYPE
("Something Asserted About or Derived From an Entity Type")

Fact Type Name (Singular Noun):

Object Type Name[1]:

Domain/Class[1]:

Required (Yes/No)?

Derivation Method[2]:

Example(s):

[1]e.g., Unary Fact (Attribute), Derived Fact, Asserted Fact, Semi-Derived Fact
[2]e.g., Count, Sum, Compute

ROLE TYPE
("A Role-Based Relationship Between Types")

Predicate 1 Name:
Predicate 1 Mandatory (Yes/No)?
Predicate 1 Unique (Yes/No)?
Predicate 1 Constraint(s)[1]:
Predicate 2 Name:
Predicate 2 Mandatory (Yes/No)?
Predicate 2 Unique (Yes/No)?
Predicate 2 Constraint(s)[1]:
Example(s):

[1]e.g., a Unique-Where-True constraint

Figure 2: Flash Cards for Object-Role Modeling.

Key Points

- Data modeling should be an interactive activity in which all project stakeholders can tell their stories about what is needed and what they are trying to accomplish. Project stakeholders need to know that their input is appreciated, that their concerns have been noted, and that they have an ownership interest in the results of the modeling activities. In this way, stakeholders are more likely to take the data model seriously and use it as part of their own project activities.

- The data modeler needs to find the particular method of interaction that will work with a particular project team. If one method isn't working, abandon it quickly and try another.

- Any given approach will be successful only insofar as it: a) engages the interests of the stakeholders involved and b) continually surfaces important information about the data requirements of the project.

- There are several ways to "start the data conversation" with stakeholders, including whiteboarding, sticky notes, spreadsheets, data flow diagrams, and UML activity, sequence, and class models.

- Starting with a "straw man" data model and including either existing canonical entities or universal data model patterns, is an excellent way to jump-start a modeling discussion.

- Other techniques for visualizing data requirements and promoting creative interactions with business users include frameworks, brainstorming, card sorting, and collages.

- Make use of techniques such as the use of shading, different font colors, and text boxes (for explanatory notes) to make your data models as communicative (and understandable) as possible.

Chapter 7
Notes on Notations

Everybody gets 12 crayons and an 8½ x 11 piece of paper.

Old Musician's Adage

By this time, you'll have noticed that all the examples in this book are in traditional Entity-Relation (E-R) data modeling notation. This is because the company I work for has standardized on a particular E-R modeling tool, and that's the tool I use. But in a book like this, I think it's helpful to take a quick look at other types of data modeling notations and their use cases.

Before I do, though, let me recap a few things: Any data model, using any type of data modeling notation, needs to be able to do the following things:

- They need to drive useful conversations about the data landscape of a particular business problem or opportunity.

- They need to bring people into agreement on the data requirements of particular projects or programs.

- They need to ensure that similar data is defined consistently across all applications and services within an organization (or at least within a business domain).

- They need to enable the rapid implementation of data as needed to support deployments of applications and services (i.e., they need to support Model-Driven Development and an Agile/DevOps application development methodology).

Always keep these requirements in mind when evaluating the pros and cons of using a particular data modeling notation in a given situation.

E-R MODELING

As I've already said, there are things I like about my E-R modeling tool and things I don't like. My tool easily switches between conceptual, logical, and physical views of data to present different information to different audiences. Making changes to models is quick and easy, which makes it possible for me to support multiple Agile projects at one time. I can easily export metadata in the form of documents or spreadsheets, and create PDFs of the models to share with project stakeholders or post to a team website. The models are easy for all project stakeholders to understand, and they don't require a lot of specialized knowledge. Finally, with some judicious use of the tool's macro language, I can export DDL for any relational DBMS from the model, exactly to my company's standards, without any manual tweaking. This allows me to turn around requested database changes quickly.

On the minus side, there's the difficulty of doing logical-to-physical transformations, the difficulty of "forward-engineering" physical models into non-relational databases, and the difficulty of interfacing with automated CI/CD tools.

There is also the issue of not being able to show complex (e.g., tertiary or n-ary) relationships without creating association entities. This is a specific example of a more general problem with relational modeling tools: too often, we end up modeling structures instead of actual business concepts! The aspect that makes these tools useful for Agile development (being able to rapidly switch between conceptual, logical, and physical views of data), can also impede our ability to model business concepts and data requirements independently from their eventual physical instantiations.

The General Ledger Account table in the case study at the end of this book is an example of this. In business terms, this table is a composite of six different business attributes, two of which are allowed to be NULL (see below). But my modeling tool won't allow me to create an entity with a compound key that includes nullable attributes! So I have to create a surrogate key, even in the logical model, and then define an Alternate Key (AK) to show the natural business key:

G/L Account

G/L Account Identifier: NOT NULL
Division Code: NOT NULL (FK) (AK1.1)
Claim Category Code: NOT NULL (FK) (AK1.2)
Dealer Division Code: NOT NULL (AK1.3)
Dealer Country Code: NOT NULL (FK) (AK1.4)
Responsibility Code: NULL (FK) (AK1.5)
Responsibility Description: NULL
Coverage Type Code: NULL (FK) (AK1.6)
Coverage Type Description: NULL
Service Materials Indicator: NOT NULL

An experienced data modeler learns to accept and work around the limitations of the modeling notations and tools. But we don't have to like it!

OBJECT-ROLE (FACT-BASED) MODELING

One alternative to E-R modeling, at least for conceptual modeling, is the fact-based or Object-Role (ORM) approach. In fact-based modeling, all attributes of entities are modeled as relationships. This permits a greater degree of semantic precision when defining business rules that involve either characteristics of attributes or relationships between attributes (neither of which are supported by E-R modeling tools).

For example, an E-R model might have an entity called *Person*, with attributes *Title* and *Gender*. But then how do you denote the business rule that if *Title* = "Mrs.", "Miss" or "Ms.", then *Gender* must be "F" (Female)? And how do you enforce the requirement that if a *Person* has a *Title* that is associated with a particular *Gender*, then that *Person* must be of that *Gender*?[45] Fact-based modeling makes it easy to specify business rules at an attribute-relationship level, as opposed to an entity-relationship level. In an E-R model, you would have to create separate entities for *Person*, *Title*, and *Gender*, and then create an associative entity to store the valid combinations of Title and Gender, and then associate the *Person* entity with the *Title/Gender* associative entity!

Fact-based conceptual models can show very complex relationships, including n-ary relationships (e.g., an *Athlete* representing a *Country* wins a *Medal* at a *Competition* in some *City* on some *Date*), subsets, inclusive and exclusive subtypes, inclusive-or and exclusive-or constraints, etc. The following page contains an example of an ORM model.[46]

However, fact-based modeling has its limitations as well. For one thing, fact-based models can become very large and unwieldy, especially for entities with many attributes. And not all attributes of an entity need to participate in relationships. The notation can be extremely complex (Appendix B of Halpin's book, which summarizes the ORM modeling notation, is nine pages long).

---

[45] See Halpin, Terry. *Object-Role Modeling Fundamentals* (New Jersey: Technics Publications, 2015), p. 7.

[46] This image is from Wikipedia.

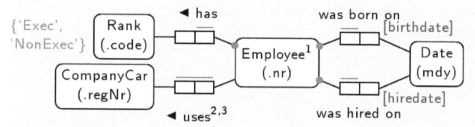

[1] **For each** Employee, birthdate $<$ hiredate.
[2] **Each** Employee **who** has Rank 'NonExec' uses **at most one** CompanyCar.
[3] **Each** Employee **who** has Rank 'Exec' uses **some** CompanyCar.

There is also the difficulty of translating an ORM model into something that can be implemented physically. The NORMA freeware tool allows you to physically map an ORM model into either relational tables or XML, but this mapping must be done manually. Since the objects in an ORM model may be either entities or attributes (the modeler doesn't have to decide which), this determination must be made at mapping time, and proper names must be assigned. In any event, complex business rules would have to be implemented as code (either in application code or perhaps as database triggers).

Fact-based modeling is useful when precisely defining the semantics of data properties and business rules is necessary (it's used, for example, by the European Space Agency). But it may be overkill for normal business applications. Remember what I said before, that effective communication with stakeholders is not necessarily a matter of precise semantics!

Graph Modeling

Graph modeling is another alternative to E-R modeling. Like fact-based modeling, graph modeling depicts attributes as relationships, and these relationships are expressed in the form of a directed graph (also known as a *concept map*). Here is an example[47]:

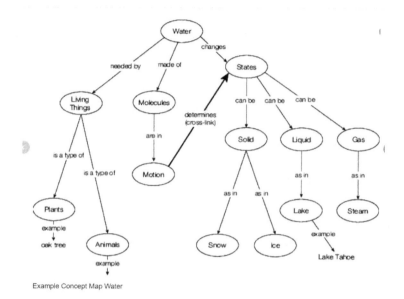

Example Concept Map Water

In graph models, entities are depicted by ovals and associated attributes are shown as rounded rectangles. Specific examples of attribute values are denoted by sharp rectangles. Connecting lines show 1-1 (straight lines) or 1-Many (directed arrows) relationships.

Graph models are very easy to understand and useful for conceptual modeling for a business audience. However, as with fact-based modeling, graph models become unwieldy when trying to create logical models with many attributes, and they are difficult to translate into implementable physical models. Very complex models can be managed by creating a high-level overview model and then "exploding" it into layers of more detailed models. You can also turn a concept map into a property graph where attributes appear in boxes next to entities:

---

[47] This image is from Wikipedia.

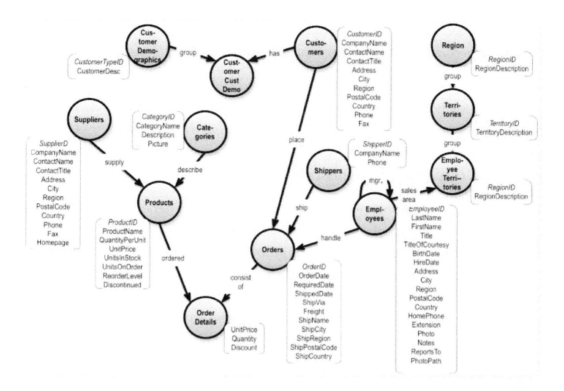

Graph modeling should be considered when the physical instantiation of the data will be in a graph database (like Neo4j), or a key-value pair database.

UML Class Modeling

The Unified Modeling Language (UML) is a library of different models used in designing and building object-oriented (O-O) applications. I've made reference to some of them (e.g., sequence, state, and activity diagrams) in this book.

UML Class Models, like E-R models, capture relationships between entities (called Object Classes in UML) and record attributes as characteristic properties. They differ from E-R models in two important respects: First, UML class models are not necessarily normalized—an object class contains all the attributes needed to support the class's operations (activities). Second, object classes contain methods (processes they can initiate) and attributes (properties). UML class models are process-oriented rather than data-oriented.[48]

UML has a rich assortment of constructs, including stereotypes, static and dynamic classification, aggregation, composition, association, derivations, classification, generalization, etc. It is very good at representing complex datatypes. UML models also arguably better than E-R models at separating specification (requirements) from implementation.

There are, however, problems with the use of UML as a data modeling tool. As we've seen, in UML class models, you are not really modeling data requirements—rather, you are modeling object requirements. The intention of UML is to communicate software architecture requirements rather than data or process requirements. When data is thought of merely in terms of object properties, important data requirements and business data rules can be ignored. And since everything has to be defined in terms of object classes, it's difficult to model business concepts or requirements that can't be defined in terms of these structures.[49]

It is best to use UML class models when the data is going to be implemented in an object database or similar persistence store.

Here is an example of a UML class model:

---

[48] As Martin Fowler puts it, "The major problem in using class diagrams is that it is easy to develop a class model that is data-oriented rather than being responsibility-oriented." *UML Distilled*, p. 8.

[49] Ted Hills makes this point in his book *NoSQL and SQL Data Modeling* (New Jersey: Technics Publications, 2016), p. 62.

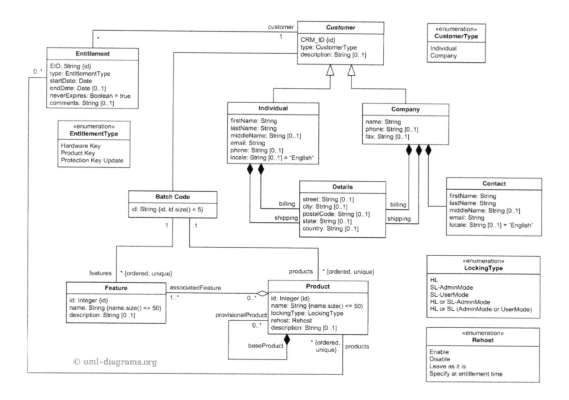

© uml-diagrams.org

COMN Modeling

The Concept and Object Modeling Notation (COMN) is another semantics-based modeling language that is geared to NoSQL databases. COMN supports a high degree of precision in the specification of data requirements, as well as separating the specification of real-world concepts from the specification of their instantiation in a database or software object.[50]

COMN models make it easy to trace the specification of requirements from the conceptual (business) model to the logical (specification) model to the physical (instantiation) model, and the physical model can be almost any type of DBMS,

---

[50] Ted Hills' book *NoSQL and SQL Data Modeling* (New Jersey: Technics Publications, 2016) is an excellent reference to the COMN modeling approach.

including relational, NoSQL, hybrid, document, key-value, etc. Many sorts of complex datatypes, including nested datatypes, arrays, hierarchies, and subsets, can be modeled.

As with other semantically-focused modeling languages, the notation can be abstruse. There is also (at present) a lack of vendor support for tools that can create COMN models and auto-generate the database instantiations from the physical model.[51] This is essential for doing model-driven development.

SUMMARY

Most of the various approaches to modeling data requirements have a few things in common. First, they all acknowledge three different types of models:

- *Conceptual models*, which are used to specify real-world business concepts, requirements and rules.

- *Logical models*, which are used to more precisely specify data requirements and organization, irrespective of any physical implementation.

- *Physical models*, which specify the precise physical instantiation of the data.

Different modeling approaches use different terms for these three levels of modeling. Thomas Frisendal, for example, refers to them as concept models, solution models, and physical models.[52] But the concepts are similar across all the notations.

---

[51] The modeling examples in Ted Hills' book appear to have been done in Visio.

[52] Frisendal, Thomas. *Graph Data Modeling for SQL and NoSQL* (New Jersey: Technics Publications, 2016).

As you can see from the descriptions above, some notations are more focused on one or two of these model types. ORM, for example, is more suited to conceptual models, while UML is more geared toward physical models. Some notations, such as COMN, do a better job of creating a strict separation (with traceability) between the three modeling types. Some notations, such as E-R and graph models, have better tool support for rapidly implementing data models into physical structures.

From the standpoint of "Data Model Storytelling", data models need to follow the essential characteristics of good design. As Don Norman puts it, two of the most important characteristics of good design are *discoverability* and *understanding*.[53] Does the model clearly communicate its intent, and make it easy for people to understand not only what the model is saying, but also what to do about it? A well-designed data model should lead people down easy-to-understand pathways of insight and understanding, like pathways through a garden. As I pointed out in *Growing Business Intelligence*, nobody needs a user manual to understand what to do in a garden!

Data models should enable stakeholders to specify data requirements and model them in a way that accurately depicts those specifications and facilitates discussion and agreement. It should also be possible for stakeholders to easily validate that the model accurately captures the specifications. Further, it should be possible to quickly and easily translate conceptual (business) specifications to logical (data) specifications to physical (database) specifications without a lot of time-consuming manual work.

Regardless of the modeling approach or nomenclature used, these requirements are key to creating models that provide immediate and lasting value to the business, especially in an Agile or DevOps development environment!

---

[53] Norman, Don. *The Design of Everyday Things* (Philadelphia: Perseus Books Group, 2013), p. 3.

Key Points

- All data modeling notations have strengths, weaknesses, and limitations. However, any data model, using any type of data modeling notation, needs to be able to do the following things:

  - They need to accurately capture important conceptual information about a business problem, domain, or opportunity.

  - They need to accurately capture business data requirements and data rules and ensure that similar data is defined consistently across an organization (or at least a business domain).

  - They need to facilitate discussion and bring people into agreement regarding data requirements and their eventual implementation.

  - They need to be easy to validate to ensure that the model accurately captures the specification of the requirements.

  - They need to make it easy to translate requirements from the conceptual (business) level to the logical (data) level to the physical (database) level so that new and changing business requirements can be quickly turned into value-producing functionality.

- The various modeling tools and approaches work best for particular types of modeling (conceptual vs. logical vs. physical), so some compromising will be necessary to make a Model-Driven Development (MDD) approach work using any given tool.

- Also, some tools are more geared toward the instantiation of data in particular types of databases (relational, graph, document, key-value, etc.). Often, the choice of a target architecture or DBMS will dictate which tool and notation to use (this shouldn't be the case, but it often is).

Chapter 8
Data Modeling and Process Stories

Storytelling is the most powerful way to put ideas into the world.

Robert McKee

Throughout my career in data management, I've concentrated on exploring ways that data professionals can add value to the organizations they work in. As every data professional knows, it is often a challenge to convince management that investing in quality data and in quality data processes will generate a worthwhile return. So, I look for every opportunity to suggest data initiatives that can generate significant ROI (Return On Investment) for organizations.

One area in which data professionals can add value is Business Process Management (BPM). As envisioned and advocated by people like Peter Drucker, Michael Hammer, James Champy, and Thomas Davenport, BPM (also known as Business Process Reengineering) involves re-imagining the way in which a business works, rejecting assumptions that may have been made in the past about what sort of work is needed and how this work should be done, and creating streamlined or entirely new processes that deliver more business value more quickly.

Data professionals can, and should, be part of this effort. I have always maintained that a logical data model tells the story of a business and how it interacts with its stakeholders. If, for example, you were to look at a data model from my company, you would most likely not see any entity called "Customer", which would strike you as strange until you saw the prominent, central location of the entity called "Dealer". This would tell you that we sell our products and services through a network of OEMs. And, if you were really imaginative, you might start thinking about whether there were products or services you might be able to sell directly to customers (without, of course, undercutting your OEMs!).

I give some examples of this in my book, *Building the Agile Database*. Cabela's, the sporting goods company, sells most of its products in its stores. But it offers discounts to preferred customers directly via email on items that are being closed out of inventory. An even more significant example is American Hospital Supply (AHS), which buys medical supplies from its suppliers and resells them to doctor's offices and hospitals. AHS completely reimagined its operations by creating an online portal that allows its customers to order directly from its suppliers! At first glance, this seems crazy; why cut out the "middleman" when that "middleman" is your own company! However, there is wisdom in this apparent madness. First of all, the company recognized that a transformation of this sort was inevitable, given the way that consumers have embraced the Internet, and knew they needed to get in front of this change and help direct it. Second, they made sure the revamped process generated revenue by charging customers a monthly fee for using the portal, and charging suppliers a percentage of each order. Third, AHS saves a lot of money by not needing to maintain a warehouse and inventory of products and by not having to ship products to customers.

Using Data Flow Diagrams (DFDs)

So how can data professionals contribute meaningfully to the reengineering (I prefer to say, *reimagining*) of business processes? The first and most important thing to keep in mind is that an organization's data does not consist of static data entities, as we are accustomed to seeing in data models, but rather of data *process flows* that move data from place to place (oftentimes undergoing transformations along the way). Most data professionals know how to create logical data models, but only a small percentage know how to create Data Flow Diagrams (DFDs), which document the process flows associated with data stores. Here is an example of a DFD:

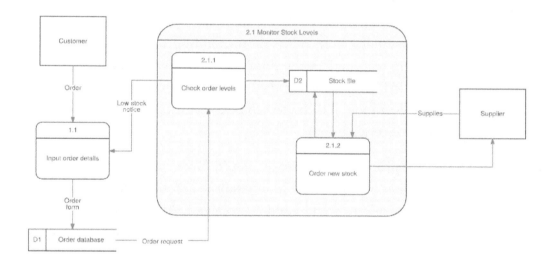

A Logical Data Model (LDM) can (and should) inspire managers to envision new ways of using and leveraging data. Managers should be able to look at a data model and think, "What could we do with this data?" An LDM is analogous to an inventory of an organization's data assets.

But a DFD should spark conversations about how the interactions between data and processes can be made more efficient or more value-producing. The book *Reengineering the Corporation*[54] gives the example of Ford's revamp of its

---

[54] Hammer, Michael and James Champy. *Reengineering the Corporation: A Manifesto for Business Revolution* (HarperCollins Publications, 1993), pp. 40-44.

procurement process.[55] The old procurement process required the purchasing department to send a purchase order to a vendor, with a copy going to accounts payable. When the vendor shipped the goods, a record would be created at the receiving dock and sent to accounts payable. The vendor, meanwhile, sent accounts payable an invoice for the goods. If all three documents (the purchase order, the receiving document, and the invoice) matched, accounts payable would send a check. The revised procurement process works like this: a buyer enters an order into a database, which records the order and forwards it to the vendor. The vendor sends the goods. At the receiving dock, a worker checks the database to make sure there is an order corresponding to the shipment. If so, receipt of the goods is recorded in the database, and a check to the vendor is automatically scheduled. If not, the goods are returned to the vendor. In other words, payment authorization, which used to be performed by accounts payable, is now handled at the receiving dock!

A DFD of Ford's old procurement process would have surfaced the realization that if order information was available in a database accessible to workers at the receiving dock, those workers could validate received shipments against orders directly, rather than sending receiving documents to accounts payable for verification.

David R. Vincent makes the point that in the new global economy, business value is created by establishing and nurturing *relationships* with customers, suppliers, dealers, and other stakeholders. He further points out that the essence of effective relationships lies in *empowerment*; in giving people the ability to do more things for themselves.[56] Hammer and Champy point out that the

---

[55] One fundamental principle of BPM is that you can't reengineer business departments or functions, such as accounts receivable or accounts payable. You can only reengineer business *processes*, such as procurement. A business process always has one or more inputs and one or more outputs.

[56] Vincent, David R. *The Information-Based Corporation: Stakeholder Economics and the Technology Investment* (Dow Jones-Irwin, 1990).

reengineering of Ford's procurement process would not be possible without the database that gives receiving dock workers access to purchase orders. In other words, data (and information) acts as an *essential enabler*. Data and information also act as *essential disrupters*; Hammer and Champy note that customers have gained the upper hand in their relationships with sellers, in part because customers now have easy access to enormously more data.[57] The popularity of online ordering through Amazon, for example, can be explained by the ease with which consumers can compare products and prices side-by-side to get the best deal.

"True" Stories vs. "Good" Stories

All too often, data modelers (and process modelers) document the existing data structures and data flows without recognizing whether they may be artifacts of outdated assumptions and inefficient processes. Data professionals are often not regarded as value-producing because they are seen as merely the documenters of the status quo and not as recognizers (or advocates) of the possibilities for transformative change. Data professionals should always be asking the question, "Is this what we *ought* to be doing?", along with the follow-on question, "Is there a better way to do this?" We should always recognize, document, and challenge assumptions that may be outdated and processes that may have been rendered inefficient or irrelevant by advances in technology. We should always be looking for ways to use data-driven technology to transform how organizations interact with their stakeholders and achieve success. For example, I once created a data model to support the reengineering of a decades-old mainframe-based process for supplying parts specifications to suppliers; the improved process (and the application created to support it) resulted in the saving of weeks of time getting customized parts from the manufacturers to our assembly lines.

---

[57] Reengineering the Corporation, p. 20.

Michael Hammer cautions that technology, improperly applied, can be a hindrance to reengineering by "reinforcing old ways of thinking and old behavior patterns."[58] Data professionals need to keep this caution in mind, particularly when using data model design patterns. Data model patterns are often useful in keeping data modelers from continually "reinventing the wheel" when solving data problems, but use data model patterns *mindfully*. We need to be asking ourselves, "Does the current problem require the same solution as before, or does this problem need to be rethought, and its solution re-imagined?"

This brings us to an aspect of reengineering that Hammer and Champy express in the following way: "Find the long-standing rule or rules that technology allows the company to break, then see what business opportunities are created by breaking those rules."[59] Data professionals need to ask themselves the following questions:

- Where are the logjams and bottlenecks in our current data management processes?

- What (perhaps) out-of-date assumptions are constraining our data management vision?

- Where does disruptive technology exist that we can use to transform these processes?

- What value might be produced by reengineering these processes?

In *Building the Agile Database*, I noted two particular challenges for modern-day data managers:

1) Business and IT stakeholders (including developers, scrum masters, QA testers, application architects, and project managers) do not

---

[58] Reengineering the Corporation, p. 83.

[59] Reengineering the Corporation, p. 91.

always understand the value of data management practices (such as data modeling).

2) Data management processes often don't mesh well with current application development methodologies such as Agile and DevOps.

PRINCIPLES OF PROCESS REENGINEERING

So now let's ask the question: "How can we reengineer *data management* processes to create end-user value and streamline development processes?" Hammer and Champy (along with David R. Vincent) give us the following guidelines for finding an answer to this question:

- Identify and challenge the assumptions upon which the old ways of doing things have been built.

- Identify and make use of disruptive technologies.

- Empower stakeholders to do as much of the work as possible.

- Reduce "handoffs" between tasks in a process (where one group of stakeholders is waiting on another for input or information).

- Optimize the process as a whole rather than improving individual tasks.

- Focus on *outputs,* not artifacts (for example, the "output" of the data modeling process is not the data model artifact; it is the shared understanding of the data requirements among project stakeholders).

- Show tangible results *quickly.*

A reengineering effort should always start with a *vision.* When John Martin, the CEO of Taco Bell, started his company's reengineering efforts in the early 1980s, he was determined to create "a vision of Taco Bell as a giant in the fast-food industry – not just the leader in the Mexican category, but a competitive force with which all restaurant organizations in all categories would have to contend."[60]

This vision led Martin to move Taco Bell out of its traditional brick-and-mortar stores into corporate and industrial dining centers, schools and universities, airports, and stadiums. Since 1989, Taco Bell's sales have increased by 22 percent per year!

When I taught business school, I would always tell my students that assumptions constrain ambitions—our assumptions of what is and isn't possible to do. If the railroad companies at the turn of the 20th Century had thought of themselves as providers of transportation services, rather than as operators of trains, we could all be flying today on Great Northern Airlines!

REENGINEERING DATA MANAGEMENT

So what might the "reengineering" of data management look like? In *Building the Agile Database*, I presented the following principles for doing Agile data management:

1) Data management must be done in a way that ensures the success of projects and project stakeholders.

2) The project team (not the data modeler) owns the data model and all related DM artifacts.

3) The project team (or designated team members) are active participants in the DM process.

---

[60] Reengineering the Corporation, pp. 173, 179.

4) Data models and other DM artifacts are updated and used continuously throughout the project (and afterward) by all members of the project team.

5) DM artifacts are used not only to identify and document project requirements but also to *implement* some subset of the solution.

Keep in mind the statement mentioned above from David R. Vincent that "the essence of effective relationships lies in *empowerment*; in giving people the ability to do more things for themselves." This is the basis for how we should reengineer data management; by giving our end users and project stakeholders more direct involvement in DM processes such as data modeling and master data management. What we want to do is eliminate the perception of data work as a process where requirements are handed off to a data modeler who then goes into a cave for several days (or weeks) and then surfaces with a data model diagram that can't be changed (or that can be changed only with significant difficulty and delays). In order for end-users and project stakeholders to see value in data models, they must feel as though they are *their* data models and that they reflect the story they want to tell.

So what should the "reengineering vision" for data management be? In *Building the Agile Database*, I suggested the following maxim, given to me by a former professor:

> *The right data*
> *To the right person*
> *At the right time*
> *In the right form*
> *At a cost that yields value.*

But our goal should be more than this. Throughout my career in data management, my personal goal has been to do my work in such a way that, at the end of each project, the project stakeholders would say, "This project would not have succeeded without the data work that was done." I am pleased to say that our management has recognized this value, and that I have been asked to do the data management work (which encompasses everything from data architecture to data modeling to database development, data cleansing, data integration, and data migration) on most of our Tier 1 application development projects.

In other words, I want data management to be viewed as more than just a "necessary evil", something that no one really wants but feels as though it ought to be done. I want data management to be viewed as the *principal enabler* of significant change and value creation at all levels of the organization!

The second step in the reengineering process is to examine assumptions and old ways of doing things that constrain our ability to adapt to change and take advantage of new opportunities. What assumptions are we bringing to our DM work that hampers our ability to create value?

The first such assumption, I would say, is that data management is something that can only be done meaningfully at an enterprise level. That is to say, that data management must always encompass the totality of an organization's data assets in order to be meaningful. This has the effect of making data management almost irrelevant (not to mention unworkable) at a project or program level. A point I often make is this: If data management is viewed as solely an enterprise-level practice, then it will be perceived as having value only at the strategic enterprise level, and will not be perceived as contributing value to the day-to-day business-level and IT-level work.[61]

---

61 This is not to say that project-level data modeling doesn't draw from, and contribute to, higher-level models such as canonical, domain and enterprise data models; I'm just saying that modeling work needs to be perceived as having value at the project or program level as well as at the Enterprise level.

In *Growing Business Intelligence*, I introduced a landscaping concept called "working toward".[62] You don't create an entire landscape all at once, you build it up in small projects over time, working toward a vision of what you want the landscape to look like and what you want it to do. In *Building the Agile Database*, I recommended doing DM work at the business subject area level (e.g., inventory management, accounts payable, order processing), and this approach gels more-or-less with a new approach being taken to application development called *Domain-Driven Development* (more on this in a later chapter). So, rather than starting with a complete enterprise data model (which would be out-of-date before you even completed it), you might rather choose to do a quick conceptual model at the enterprise level (a sort of high-level overview), and then flesh it out on a project-by-project basis by creating an interconnected set of subject-area or domain models (each of which would add significant value to one or more projects or programs).[63]

The second assumption to challenge is that data management is an esoteric discipline that only highly-trained specialists can do and that business and IT front-line workers don't have the necessary training and expertise to participate in DM practices. Obviously, a certain amount of education and training is necessary to succeed in any discipline, but do not assume that business and IT staffers are unwilling or unable to understand and participate in DM work. Over the years, the data group where I work has conducted several classes called "Clear Thinking About Data" (CTAD) at business units all over our organization, teaching the basic principles of data modeling to business users so that they can better manage their own data (and participate more fully in data modeling

---

[62] Burns, Larry. *Growing Business Intelligence* (Technics Publications, 2016), pp. 33-34.

[63] David Hay, in his book *Achieving Buzzword Compliance*, describes a high-level "overview" conceptual model which supports multiple "semantic" models (each describing an area of the business). These are what I think of as business subject area (or Domain) models. Finally, he describes "essential" models which pull together divergent viewpoints from the various semantic models, crossing business area boundaries. I use the term Canonical to describe these types of data models.

efforts on projects that affect their business units). We have also taught classes in data modeling, database design, and database development (including SQL coding) to application developers as part of a series of discussions called "Database Information Exchange" (DBIX[64]). These classes not only help application developers participate more fully in the data work of software development projects; they also help our data people understand the challenges of application development, learn new development tools, techniques and methodologies, and hear the concerns of developers about how our data practices impact (and sometimes hinder) their development work. Without such two-way education and communication, it is impossible for DM practitioners, application developers, and business users to work together effectively on projects.

The next step in reengineering is to see what disruptive technology exists that can help remove barriers to change. I don't want to get too prescriptive here, but the following general categories of technology should certainly be explored:

- *Collaboration technology*, which allows groups of people to work together from different locations at the same time. This includes the ability for multiple people to update the same document (in the same location) at the same time.

- *DevOps technology*, also known as Continuous Integration/Continuous Deployment (CI/CD), which allows project teams to update individual portions of an application solution as needed, and then automatically test and deploy those changes. This promotes rapid turnaround in responding to continually changing application requirements.

- *Cloud technology*, which provides easy and inexpensive availability to a number of foundational technologies, including the ability to easily

---

[64] We decided that the acronym 'DIE' didn't really convey the positive, uplifting image we wanted.

create servers, databases, data integrations, and process flows as needed to support an application. The cost is usually usage-based, meaning that you pay only for what you use, when you use it.

- *Services technology,* including microservices and Enterprise Service Bus (ESB) technology. Services allow you to create mostly independent applets that talk to one another over a services hub. When canonical data is needed to support multiple applets, these data structures can reside on the ESB Hub and be used by multiple services. Data in these canonical data structures can be refreshed periodically from a Master Data Management (MDM) repository, if your organization has one.

The challenge here for data management professionals is that many of our traditional tools (e.g., data modeling tools) have not kept up with changing times. For example, I've been able to use my modeling tool's built-in macro language to create templates that allow me to deploy data models to Cloud-based DBMSs such as AWS Aurora (MySQL) and Snowflake. But there is no current integration between my modeling tool and CI/CD tools that would allow me to check in a data model and have the corresponding DDL automatically generated and deployed. This is still required to be a manual step.

After evaluating the technology options, we need to look at how to flatten hierarchies, remove rigid boundaries between different roles/groups, and reduce the number of "handoffs" required to get a given piece of work done. One way I've done this in our organization is to "deformalize" the process of making data model and database changes. Rather than making project teams submit formal requests for changes, I've taken one or more of the following approaches:

- Updating the data model directly (using a projection screen or collaboration software) during requirements, analysis, or design sessions with team members, then generating the DDL from the updated model to immediately apply the changes to the development database.

- Receiving requests from team members for database changes via email or IM. After evaluating the request (usually checking with business stakeholders or application architects to make sure the request makes sense), I will oftentimes make the database changes first (if they are simple) to unblock the dev team and then update the data model later. I will update the data model first and then generate the DDL for the database changes for more complex changes.

- In circumstances when I'm not available, developers can make changes in the development database on their own so that development isn't impeded. The caveat is that they must submit these changes for review at the earliest possible opportunity and agree to any necessary refactoring if the changes need to be modified in any way. In some cases, I may agree to allow this refactoring to be done in a subsequent sprint in order to allow the team to reach their current sprint goals successfully. This entails more work on my part since I need to make sure that the data model and the database eventually get back in synch, but it removes a roadblock to development. If the developers have been sufficiently trained in some basic data modeling techniques, and informed of our organization's data naming standards, this approach is not as risky as might be thought.

I also do the work of integrating project-level data model changes with higher-level domain and canonical models asynchronously, so that this work doesn't interfere with the cadence of sprint delivery. The general idea is to deliver what's needed to the project teams as quickly as possible and do whatever else is needed after the fact.

Finally, we must *reimagine* the outputs (results) of our data processes and ensure that they deliver significant value quickly to all levels of the organization. The central tenet of reengineering is to focus on *processes* as a whole (which take in inputs, transform these inputs in some way, and deliver outputs) rather than focusing on individual tasks or functions (like data modeling). We tend to think of the outputs of data management as artifacts, as the cells in the *Data* (or *What*) column of the Zachman Framework. But, as I like to point out, the purpose of the Zachman Framework is not to produce artifacts (i.e., documents); it's to facilitate the understanding of requirements and the successful completion of agreed-upon work! In other words, the purpose of architecture is not to produce blueprints; it's to produce a house - a house that matches the home-buyers expectations.

So, what should be the *outputs* of our data management processes? Here are some suggestions:

- A shared understanding of an organization's data assets that can drive meaningful conversations about how to leverage data and information to create value.

- Continuous improvement of an organization's business processes (including improvements in organizational reporting and data analytics).

- Continuous improvement of an organization's IT processes (including application development and data delivery).

- Continuous improvement of an organization's data assets, including improvements in data quality, breadth (acquiring useful data from outside sources to add to existing data), and availability.

- Continuous integration of data management processes with both business and IT processes.

In other words, in the same way that the goal of architects and builders is to provide their clients with houses that meet their needs at an affordable price, the goal of data professionals is to facilitate the creation and deployment of data and information assets in a way that allows organizations to quickly create value for their stakeholders. The various artifacts of data management, including data models and data flow diagrams, are the means to this end, and not the end, themselves.

CAVEATS FOR REENGINEERING

Before I conclude this topic, let me throw out a couple of caveats about the reengineering of data management processes: First, it's important to make sure you're not merely trading one set of problems for another, different, set of problems. For example, a number of organizations have rushed to replace their existing relational databases with "NoSQL" databases, to save the cost and trouble of defining data requirements ahead of application development. But this merely trades one set of costs for a different set of costs, since data quality still needs to be ensured somehow, information about canonical data (and its whereabouts) still needs to be made available to business users, and data still needs to be accessible to end-users. Similarly, moving data from on-prem to the cloud saves server and maintenance costs, but can add to development costs and increase the cost (and difficulty) of data access by end-users. So think carefully about the potential problems and costs your "target end state" may present you!

This brings me to the second caveat: make sure you're not just "kicking the can down the road" when reengineering. In the section on domain-driven development, I make the point that defining data solely at the domain level doesn't eliminate the problem of canonical data, it merely defers it. At some point, when applications in multiple domains need access to the same (cross-domain) data, you are either going to have to create canonical data structures, figure out how to populate them, and then refactor applications and services to use them, or you're going to have to create duplicate, redundant, data structures in multiple domains and figure out how to keep the data in synch. Eliminating up-front application development costs may lead to greater costs (and more work) down the road.

The third caveat, which I've mentioned before, is: make sure your "reengineering" effort isn't just streamlining or enabling archaic ways of doing things. Automating a buggy-whip factory isn't going to do much good once everybody is driving cars!

In *Growing Business Intelligence*, I make the point that process reengineering should not only identify a goal and move toward it, but also identify an obstacle and remove it.[65] Each process we reengineer should not simply accomplish a unit of work, but should do so in a way that makes further repetition of that work unnecessary (or at least faster and easier to do the next time). For example, in gardening we don't want to have to weed the same area of the garden over and over again. So after we weed a section, we cover it with plastic or newspapers (weighted down with rocks) or with "smother mulch" (mounds of wood chips, leaves or straw). This kills the weeds in that section of the garden, and annual mulching will keep the weeds away. So don't just reengineer to make weeding faster and easier. Try to make the entire process of weeding unnecessary!

There is probably much more that needs to be said (and written) on the subject of reengineering data management, but this should give DM practitioners something to think about, to improve DM processes at their own organizations.

---

[65] *Growing Business Intelligence*, p. 70.

Key Points

- Data models, DFDs, and other data-related artifacts can be extremely useful in supporting organizational BPR (business process reengineering) efforts.

- Data modelers need to do more than simply document an organization's existing data assets and business processes; they need to ask, "What *should* the organization be doing?" and, "Is there a better way to do this?"

- Make sure the data model is not just telling a *true* story (about an organization's vision, mission, and values), but also a *good* story (that is, make sure the data model supports and enables future organizational growth).

- BPR focuses on end-to-end processes (e.g., application database development, data governance, MDM, etc.), rather than specific tasks (like data modeling).

- All processes consist of inputs, transformations, and outputs. Start by asking yourself what the outputs of a particular process ought to be, and work backward from there.

- Make sure you're not just automating archaic processes, enabling the wrong behavior, trading one set of problems for another, or "kicking the can down the road" (i.e., deferring work that needs to be done eventually).

- A BPR effort should always begin with a vision of the value that a particular process ought to contribute to an organization.

- Identify and challenge the assumptions upon which the old ways of doing things have been built. Identify and use disruptive technologies; and empower stakeholders to do as much of the work as possible.

- Just as data modeling and other data-related activities can contribute to an organization's process reengineering efforts, we can also apply the principles of BPR to improve our data-related processes and the value they contribute.

Section II
Agile Data, Revisited

In any given moment, we have two options: to step forward into growth or to step back into safety.

Abraham Maslow

I've written a great deal about Agile Data in my two previous books, *Building the Agile Database* and *Growing Business Intelligence*. At this point, though, I'd like to give us all a level-set about what Agile Data is (and isn't), and why it's important to data professionals.

What follows is an overview and summary of my approach to Agile Data, the reasoning underlying the Agile approach, and some ways in which we, as data practitioners, can take a more Agile approach to our data work.[66]

It's important that data professionals understand the *technology context* and (for want of a better word) the *human context* of a project, as well as the *business context* and the *data context*.

---

[66] Note: the material in this Section is taken mostly from my Agile Data Workshop, which I've done in several cities. Some of this material may duplicate material already presented in the previous Section, but I'm including it in this Section for completeness.

On the technology side, we need to understand things like what sort of data persistence and data transport mechanisms will be used, so we can better understand what support will be needed from us.[67] Also, we should understand how application and data integration, deployment and testing will be done, and how our work will be integrated into the final solution product.

On the human side, we need to understand our stakeholders and develop strategies for working effectively with them. There may be personality conflicts (some people are easier to work with than others), or there may be logistical difficulties if some team members are working remotely.[68]

On the business side, of course, we need to understand the business requirements of the project, especially the business data requirements, and we also need to understand the value the business expects to see from the finished product.

And, of course, we need to understand the data context of the project. Is data going to be migrated from existing data sources to a new repository? Does the application need to integrate data from multiple existing sources? Are there data quality concerns, and if so, how will they be mitigated? Are there data security concerns? If so, how will they be addressed?

Try to keep these four contexts in mind when applying the principles described in this section to your particular project or situation. And remember that any truly Agile solution will be:

- *Cooperative* – including all affected stakeholders in the process.

---

[67] For example, on one project that made extensive use of web services, I spent a lot of time modeling and creating XML schema definitions for data transport. On my current project, the application made extensive use of *delegated tables*, which allow users to upload data directly into the application from spreadsheets.

[68] This has been of particular significance over the last year or so, because of the Covid-19 pandemic. Companies and organizations have had to be creatively focused on keeping their remote workers engaged, productive and optimistic.

- *Dynamic* – continually improving in response to changing needs and new technologies.
- *Exploratory* – looking for new ways of delivering value.
- *Flexible* – open to new ways of doing things.
- *Reusable* – able to be leveraged to solve future problems.
- *Sustainable* – delivering continual value over time with less and less effort.

Chapter 9
What Agile Is and Isn't

> *Cooperation is the thorough conviction that nobody can get there unless everybody gets there.*
>
> Virginia Burden

I've written about Agile quite a bit over the years, and I've described my approach to Agile development in both of my previous books, *Building the Agile Database* and *Growing Business Intelligence*.[69] I've used both home remodeling and landscape gardening as metaphors to describe my approach to Agile, because this is how almost everybody on Earth approaches any complex undertaking:

1. We start with a vision of what the end result of the project will look like.

2. We take the first few steps toward the realization of the vision.

3. We then reassess our end goal in light of what we've accomplished so far.

4. We assess our progress to date, and figure out ways of improving our efforts.

---

[69] Burns, Larry. *Growing Business Intelligence* (New Jersey: Technics Publications, 2016).

5. We take the next few steps toward our goal.

6. We repeat Steps 3-5 until we get to a point that may not look exactly like our original vision, but is where we are satisfied enough to call the project complete.

When I first started writing about Agile,[70] I commented on the fact that Agile is a term that you almost never encounter outside of IT. You never, for example, hear anyone describe themselves as Agile Carpenters or Agile Plumbers or Agile Bankers or Agile CPAs. Why is this? I believe it's because everybody on Earth, outside of IT, knows how work is supposed to be done!

The Agile community itself seems to be coming around to this same perception of Agile as a natural human process (as opposed to yet another IT-centric application development methodology). Dave Thomas, one of the principal authors of the "Agile Manifesto",[71] now advocates abandoning the concept of Agile (as a noun or an adjective) in favor of the concept of Agility (as a verb). Thomas' approach to Agility[72] reads very much like the "do it yourself" process I described above:

- Find out where you are.
- Take a small step towards your goal.
- Adjust your understanding based on what you learned.
- Repeat.

In other words, as I've said before, Agile is not so much a defined methodology as much as it is a way of working (or of thinking about working). As Dave

---

[70] I wrote a number of feature columns on Agile Data for TDAN (The Data Administration Newsletter) from 2005 to 2013. You can find them at TDAN.com.

[71] "Manifesto for Agile Software Development", www.agilemanifesto.org.

[72] Thomas, Dave. "Agile is Dead (Long Live Agility). Blog posting, March 4, 2014. https://bit.ly/3gAhtwa.

Thomas puts it, we don't do "Agile Development". We do Development Agilely! He makes an additional important point: ultimately, what we do trumps what we call it. Nevertheless, let's take another, deeper look at Agile and how it works.

AGILE AS WORK, RISK, AND OPPORTUNITY MANAGEMENT

The important thing to remember about Agile as a methodology is that it manages work. Specifically:

- No work is done that is not agreed to by the team.
- No work is done unless it moves the project forward.
- No work is done unless its value can be demonstrated.
- No work is done in excess of the value it creates (i.e., no "nice to have" work!).
- No work is done that is perfect (i.e., only "good enough").
- The right work must be done at the right time by the right people in the right way.
- Processes of work must be continually improved.

When you work on an Agile project, you spend a lot of time in stand-up meetings, talking about what work you did yesterday, what work you expect to do today, and what obstacles (if any) you are encountering. You spend time in meetings deciding what work will be done in a sprint. You participate in post-sprint review sessions where you talk about what went well, what went poorly, and what could be improved. All of these activities are *work-management* activities.

So why is it important to manage work? Work is managed so as to manage risk. Specifically:

- The risk of doing work that isn't needed.
- The risk of not doing work that is needed.

- The risk of delivering too little too late.
- The risk of doing work too soon.
- The risk of doing work that must be done over.
- The risk of doing the wrong kind of work.

It is the risk (and expense) of doing the wrong work that was the original impetus for the Agile Manifesto. Recall that Agile was the Developer Community's response to a litany of highly-publicized and very costly software development project failures during the 1990s. Most of these software project failures resulted from spending time and money doing work that wasn't needed, wasn't the right work, or wasn't delivered soon enough to do any good.

So why is it important to manage risk? Risk is managed to manage opportunity. Specifically, to:

- Deliver as much value to the customer as soon as possible.
- Take advantage of windows of business opportunity.
- Quickly leverage breakthroughs in technology.
- Continually improve processes and business delivery.
- Continually improve quality.
- Incrementally grow knowledge, expertise, and capability.

In other words, Agile manages work to maximize opportunity and minimize risk. Or, to put it another way, Agile manages work so that opportunity isn't swallowed up by risk. Agile always intends to achieve an acceptable balance of risk (what we currently don't know and can't do) and opportunity (what we must know and be able to do in order to be successful).

This brings us back, full circle, to our landscaping and home-improvement metaphors. In every project we do, we have to find a way to identify and manage the most significant risks, which pose the greatest danger to the ultimate success of our project. We know there will be mistakes and rework. This is inevitable. But we need to try to forestall the worst mistakes before they occur and sink our efforts.

I provided an example of this in *Growing Business Intelligence*. It was a deck project I did for a 10-sided geodesic dome house that we lived in on Vashon Island, in Puget Sound. I needed to build a triangular deck in front of the house, with access paths on two sides of the triangle and stairs running up from the deck to a gallery across the front of the house. Here is a photo of the final project:

I'd never done a project like this before, so I started by identifying the most significant potential risk: that the house-facing side of the triangular deck would not be parallel to the house. This would mean that the staircase would be skewed (longer on one side than on the other), and the treads would have to be cut wider on one end than on the other (this would look awful).

By continually measuring the distance between the house and each end of the house-facing side of the deck as I was building it, I ensured that the finished deck would be parallel to the house. This minimized the risk of what would have been, potentially, the most costly bit of "rework" – having to either move or rebuild the deck! Many other glitches occurred during the project, but by forestalling the major risk, I was able to keep the other problems manageable (and relatively inexpensive).

Managing the one major risk meant that I didn't need to be paralyzed by the thought of all the other, minor, risks, and enabled me to pursue my end vision, confident that I could manage any other problems that arose in the course of the work. This is what Agile really is – managing the most significant risks so that you are unafraid to pursue your vision of success!

CHARACTERISTICS OF AN AGILE APPROACH

There are many different approaches to Agile (e.g., SCRUM, Lean, Kanban, XP), but each approach ensures that the following criteria for an Agile project are met:

- Deliver value to customers quickly and incrementally.
- Ensure continuous interaction with the business.
- Be transparent in communicating with all stakeholders.
- Accept continually changing requirements.
- Support experimentation (within limits).
- Ensure freedom to fail (quickly).
- Create cycles of continuous improvement.
- Work positively and collaboratively.
- Empower people to organize themselves and solve problems.

Although the *ways* in which we do these things may change over time (e.g., we are doing much more work remotely now), these are still the principles we should adhere to in order to ensure that our projects are successful. Agile is not a prescriptive methodology. It's really just a way of organizing motivated and committed individuals to work together to solve business problems!

HAVING AN "AGILE ATTITUDE"

As suggested above, Agile is really more of a mindset than a methodology. Agile doesn't tell us *how* to do work; instead, it gives us a different way of *thinking* about how work gets done.

In *Building the Agile Database,* I describe the Three Agile Attitudes[73]:

- *Commitment.* People on an Agile project need to be 100% committed to the project's success, above all other personal considerations. Just as a chain is only as strong as its weakest link, a project team is only as strong as its least-committed member. This is exemplified by the Agile concept of "pigs and chickens". A chicken may contribute eggs to a breakfast, but a pig gives her all. Similarly, we need to transition from being occasional contributors to a project (i.e., "chickens") to people committed to doing whatever is necessary to ensure the project's success (i.e., "pigs").

- *Cooperation.* People on Agile projects need to work effectively with each other to solve problems and get work done. This often means putting personal feelings aside, along with (on occasion) heartfelt convictions about how things ought to be done, in favor of reaching an agreement that allows the team to move forward. I don't object to having principles, but I like to point out that the only people who get paid for having principles are priests and rabbis. The rest of us get paid for creating business value for the companies that pay our salaries. It's fine to make an argument (if you have one) for doing things a certain way. But if that approach doesn't work for the team and is impacting the project, then it's up to you to either: a) find an acceptable and workable alternative that accomplishes the same goal, or b) accept the fact that it's not going to be done the way you like (at this time), and move on. Better to lose a battle (and if you learn something from it, it's never a loss) than to lose the war (i.e., have the project fail with your name on it).

---

[73] Building the Agile Database, Chapter 11.

- *Communication.* Agile projects are distinctive in that they involve nearly constant communication and interaction with every member of the project team. We need to learn how to communicate effectively with others (again, I recommend Toastmasters for this). It is also important for us to make ourselves as available as possible to the rest of the team to ask questions, request status updates, communicate new requirements, and get our help in solving problems. In particular, we need to be *proactive* in our communications. If, for example, there are database standards that need to be followed by developers, those standards need to be communicated at the very beginning of the project and agreed to by the project team. Absolutely *do not* drop an uncommunicated requirement or standard on the team in the middle of development! Don't jeopardize the success of the project (and your working relationships with team members) by blind-siding them.

In short, Agile is an attitude of positive, collaborative customer service and commitment to value delivery and continuous improvement. It is also a commitment to harness the power of change to deliver value to the business.

Agile is not just about doing things faster; it's about recognizing what the right things are to do. This involves, above all else, a spirit of humility, of recognizing that we don't have all the answers and are not solely responsible for the project's success. We need to recognize the value that each of our stakeholders is contributing to the project and appreciate the knowledge and insight they have.

WHAT AGILE IS NOT

Having talked a lot about what Agile is, I feel compelled to dispel a few myths by talking about what Agile is not:

- Agile doesn't mean that architecture is irrelevant. As we'll see in the next chapter, architecture is essential to the success of any project.

However, architecture shouldn't be "Big Design Up Front" (BDUF); instead, it should provide an easy-to-understand framework for organizing the project deliverables in a meaningful way to ensure that the final product is robust, scalable, performant, and easy to maintain. Good architecture should facilitate, rather than impede, speed of delivery while also serving to improve the quality of the delivered product.

- Agile doesn't mean that you can't or shouldn't do design. Again, the idea is to do enough design, at any one time, to bring the team into agreement on how a given set of requirements is going to be implemented and allow work to proceed. In Agile, architecture and design serve as the framework that guides and directs the team's work. An effective design helps remove uncertainty about how things should be done, which, in turn, reduces errors and rework and increases the overall velocity of the team.

- Agile doesn't mean that you can't or shouldn't reuse anything. Although opinions differ in the software development community on the merits and value of code reuse, it should be a general principle that anything you can reuse to deliver value more quickly should be reused. In particular, models (such as data models) should be reused to the greatest extent possible since that is a large part of the value of models. Services and APIs are also good candidates for reuse.

- Agile doesn't mean that you can't or shouldn't document anything. Just be judicious about what you choose to document and how. Don't document anything that's self-evident, and don't create documentation that will become obsolete and unused over time. The best place to document requirements is in models, maintained over time and reused, rather than just sitting in a binder on a shelf somewhere. When documenting code, don't document what the code is doing, document what the code is *supposed* to do! That way, people needing to make changes to the code will understand what the intent of the code was, even if the code itself is incorrect.

- Agile doesn't mean that quality is unimportant. It does mean that quality, like everything else on the project, is time-boxed. For any given sprint, the team has to decide what amount of work they can deliver, of a sufficiently high quality to satisfy the business users, in that sprint. Quality considerations need to be built into the project plan and into the acceptance criteria for each user story. The application architecture and overall design must ensure that high-quality deliverables are an objective of the project.

- Agile doesn't mean that data considerations are unimportant. Agile developers do tend to focus on functionality at the expense of data, especially when using methodologies such as Extreme Programming (XP). In *Building the Agile Database*, I told the story of a magazine for software developers that featured a weekly article describing the exploits of two Extreme Programmers. Every week, they would tweak one part of the application, only to break another component. Then they would fix that component, and another would break, etc., etc. This went on *every single week*, and it never occurred to them that they should stop their work, step back, and re-examine the overall application design!

Data professionals on Agile projects need to effectively communicate the importance of a good data model and good database design in forestalling the sort of problems that occurred with the time reporting application I mentioned earlier. Again, the project had user stories that described the functional requirements of the application, but important data requirements were not fully understood by all members of the project team, with very unfortunate results! Meeting data requirements on an Agile project is possible (as I will explain in the next few chapters), but it needs to be done in a certain way and with the support and cooperation of the project team.

Key Points

- Agile is not so much a methodology as it is a way of thinking about how to do work.

- In Agile, work is managed to maximize opportunity and minimize risk. The intent is to manage the most significant risks so that opportunities for success can be pursued with confidence.

- Agile involves envisioning a goal and taking small incremental steps to reach it. At each step, you evaluate both the process (to identify improvements) and the end goal (to see whether it needs to change). Then you use that knowledge to take the next few steps toward the (revised) goal, and so on.

- Agile is essentially a journey of discovery, where an organization gradually and iteratively tests the limits of its knowledge and understanding and grows them into new arenas of endeavor.

- At each iteration of an Agile process, one of two things must happen: either some piece of value is successfully delivered to business stakeholders, or else a small, quick, inexpensive, manageable failure occurs.

- People on an Agile project must have an "Agile Attitude", characterized by a commitment to the project's success, a spirit of cooperation with other project stakeholders, and a willingness to communicate proactively.

- Agile does not mean you can't (or shouldn't) do architecture and design, and it doesn't mean you can't do data management. It just means that you have to learn how to do these things differently—one that fits into the overall context of an Agile project.

Chapter 10
Agile Architecture

The room is there for the human being, not the human being for the room.

El Lissitzsky

Working on an Agile project doesn't (and shouldn't) mean that we don't have an over-arching application architecture and design. Some years ago, an Agile practitioner named Craig Larman created a stir with the following quote:[74]

Architecture is a bad metaphor. We don't construct our software like a building, we grow it like a garden.

However, as I pointed out in *Building the Agile Database*,[75] even in landscaping and gardening, a certain amount of architecture and design is necessary for

---

[74] Larman, Craig. "Large-Scale Agile Design and Architecture: Ways of Working". March 18, 2011 (www.infoq.com/articles/large-scale-agile-design-and-architecture).

[75] Building the Agile Database, pp. 56-59.

success. Too many people run to the garden store, buy some plants, and put them wherever they look pretty, only to see them die horrible deaths. Then they have to go back to the garden store and buy more plants (garden stores *love* these people!). Real landscapers make sure not to plant shade plants in the sun (or next to a steel-sided building that radiates 105-degree heat in the Summer), or put a decorative fish pond at the bottom of a slope, or put a patio in an area exposed to high winds and heavy rains, or plant trees next to a house or garage.

ADVANTAGES OF ARCHITECTURE

A well-defined application architecture benefits a project (even an Agile project) in many ways:

- It helps ensure "fitness of purpose" for the solution; that is, it ensures that the proposed solution solves the given business problem.

- It helps capture the *scope* and *constraints* of the project so that impossible, unnecessary, or impractical customer requirements are identified before work is put into implementing them. For example, a building architect may have to tell a client, "No, you can't put a six-car garage there; that's where the drain field for the septic system needs to go."

- It provides the framework or context in which the customer's requirements can be clearly understood ("Yes, that's right; I want a flagstone path to go between those two cedar trees and end at a gazebo at the back of the shade garden").

- It helps in identifying and mitigating potential risks to the success of the project. I worked on one project that failed after two years and more than five million dollars because the company's mainframe computer wasn't powerful enough to run the application, and there was no money available for an upgrade!

- It helps in prioritizing work and eliminating expensive rework. For example, in landscaping, you want to install water lines and electrical outlets first, then hardscaping (e.g., patios, walkways, and arbors), and finally, the planting beds. You don't want to have to rip out a patio because you forgot to run water lines to the sprinkler heads!

- It helps to ensure the reusability/extensibility of the solution. The most Agile solutions are those that can solve more than just one problem. A truly Agile solution can be reused to solve multiple business problems and should be easily extensible to accommodate changing business needs and conditions.

- It helps stem the proliferation of point solutions. There is nothing "Agile" about having multiple different solutions to the same business problem. This simply adds to the expense and cost of upkeep and negatively impacts the ROI (Return on Investment) of the solution.

- It helps ensure the fastest possible delivery speed by eliminating uncertainty about how a problem will be solved and keeping everybody on the same page about what work needs to be done.

- It helps ensure the lowest cost and highest benefit by eliminating impractical and overly expensive approaches at the very beginning of the project.

- It helps ensure that all the work that is done moves the project forward toward ultimately successful completion.

AGILE AND THE ZACHMAN FRAMEWORK

Larman's critique seems to be directed at John Zachman's *Framework for Enterprise Architecture* (see Figure 3), which many Agilists feel is an example of Big Design Up Front (BDUF) and impractical for Agile projects. However, properly understood, the Zachman Framework *is* an Agile framework! The rows of the Framework represent different stakeholder groups, the columns represent different types of requirements, and the cells (the intersection of each row and column) represent models in which stakeholder requirements are being captured and communicated across the project team. Each cell in the Framework represents a dialogue between two or more stakeholders (or stakeholder groups), in which requirements are being specified (and changed) and communicated so that important work will be done, and done in the right way. Each model represents an agreement between project stakeholders as to what work needs to be done to make the project a success, and how that work will be accomplished.

	Why	How	What	Who	Where	When
Contextual	Goal List	Process List	Material List	Organisational Unit & Role List	Geographical Locations List	Event List
Conceptual	Goal Relationship	Process Model	Entity Relationship Model	Organisational Unit & Role Relationship Model	Locations Model	Event Model
Logical	Rules Diagram	Process Diagram	Data Model Diagram	Role Relationship Diagram	Locations Diagram	Event Diagram
Physical	Rules Specification	Process Function Specification	Data Entity Specification	Role Specification	Location Specification	Event Specification
Detailed	Rules Details	Process Details	Data Details	Role Details	Location Details	Event Details

Figure 3: One Representation of the Zachman Framework (from Wikipedia)

It's important to understand that the artifacts in the cells of the Zachman Framework are *models*, not documents; they are being developed incrementally and change as user requirements change. They are used to capture important project requirements and communicate them to project stakeholders. And they are used to generate portions of the solution (e.g., the data model is used to generate the schema for creating the database). As long as the models are being developed and used in an Agile fashion, there is nothing about the Zachman Framework that is non-Agile. Even John Zachman himself has made clear that the intent of the Framework is not to define all the requirements of a project up-front!

Ultimately, as I indicated earlier, the true test of whether an Architecture is Agile is whether it ensures that all work that is done moves the project steadily forward to a successful conclusion.

PRINCIPLES OF AGILE ARCHITECTURE

Having made the case that architecture can be Agile and can provide significant value to Agile projects, I need to talk a bit about how architecture work can be done in an Agile fashion.

Here are some of my suggestions for Agile Architecture:

- Understand and appreciate the value that good architecture and design contribute to a project, and communicate this to the project team.

- Define architecture in terms of managing agreements between project stakeholders.

- Understand that architecture changes over time in response to new business requirements and emerging technologies.

- Adopt a "working toward" approach to architecture. Don't assume you can define it all up front. Define what you need now and work incrementally toward your ultimate goal.

- Make use of architecture and design patterns as much as possible; avoid reinventing the wheel.

- Use architecture to prioritize and direct the work that needs to be done to drive continual value for the project.

Remember, the ultimate test of whether anything is Agile is whether it creates value and contributes to the ultimate success of a project!

Key Points

- There are many benefits to a well-designed application architecture: it helps ensure fitness of purpose for the solution, captures the scope and constraints of the project, provides a framework for customer requests, helps identify and mitigate project risks, helps prioritize and direct work, helps ensure the reusability and extensibility of the solution, helps eliminate multiple point solutions for the same problem, and increases delivery speed.

- The Zachman Framework, properly understood, is a valid architectural framework for Agile. The framework rows represent stakeholder groups, the columns represent types of requirements, and the cells represent models in which stakeholder requirements are captured and communicated across the project team.

- Each cell in the Framework represents a dialogue between two or more stakeholders (or stakeholder groups). Requirements are being specified (and changed) and communicated so that important work will be done and done in the right way. Each model represents an agreement between project stakeholders as to what work needs to be done to make the project a success, and how that work will be accomplished.

- It's important to understand that the artifacts in the cells of the Zachman Framework are *models*, not documents—they are being developed incrementally and change as user requirements change.

- Adopt a "working toward" approach to Architecture, rather than trying to define it all up front, and understand that the architecture will change during the project in response to new user requirements and changing technology.

- Make use of architecture and design patterns as much as possible.

Chapter 11
Agile Data Modeling

All models are wrong, but some are useful.

George E. P. Box

We've already looked at some of the ground-level aspects of an Agile approach to data modeling. Now, let's move our sights up a bit and examine the underlying principles behind Agile data modeling.

WHAT A LOGICAL DATA MODEL IS (AND ISN'T)

We need to understand what a logical data model is (and isn't). A logical data model is the business requirements view of data, defined at the business subject area or higher. It contains business data definitions, rules, relationships, and constraints for an area of the business.

It is important to understand that logical data models are independent of any specific application, implementation, or usage of the data. A logical data model is not tied to any specific application or database. A logical data model should be able to support multiple applications and multiple instantiations and uses of the data within that business subject area.

Also, the logical data model changes only in response to changes in business data requirements (or our understanding of them). It does not change in response to application changes, except insofar as those changes reflect business requirements changes. A logical data model, for example, should not change if the length of a text field in a database is changed.

Decoupling the logical data model from specific applications and database implementations is the key to making data models Agile. Data models by themselves are easy to refactor and can be readily changed to reflect changing business requirements, accommodate new user stories, or drive discussions of data requirements. Database schemas, on the other hand, are much harder and more time-consuming to change!

Decoupling the logical model is important for other reasons too:

- Organizations have data needs that lie outside of specific application requirements. Businesses expect that business data can and will be available and usable for any business purpose, be it reporting, analytics, process improvement, quality assurance, or the development of new products and services. Data that is defined only in terms of application requirements cannot easily be used to meet the needs of the entire organization.

- Data that is used only to support a single application does not provide significant value (that is, ROI) to the organization. Data provides value to the organization only to the extent that it is reused (and reusable).

- Application data is often persisted in ways that violate the business' understanding of data definitions, rules, and constraints (as evidenced by the Timesheet example shown in the previous section).

MDD AND AGILE MODELS

For a logical data model to contribute value to an Agile project, it must be both an MDD (Model-Driven Development) model and an Agile model. The characteristics of an MDD model include:

- The model is used not just to understand or describe a problem but also to implement its solution (or part of the solution).

- The model must be used continually and pervasively throughout the project to help stakeholders understand the problem, the requirements, and the work that needs to be done. The model captures the agreements of the stakeholders regarding the work to be done.

- The model must capture important information or requirements not captured elsewhere in the project.

- The model describes some subset of the problem space for the project (e.g., the data model describes the business data requirements and constraints).

- The model must follow a standard and support design patterns.

- The model must be unambiguous, clear, and easy-to-understand.

- The model must be tested and validated.

- The model is used to generate some part of the solution.

- The model is used to support and maintain the solution after production deployment.

In addition, a model should also be an Agile model. Characteristics of an Agile model are:

- The model should be created and updated incrementally as requirements are discussed, understood, and agreed upon.

- The model should reflect the input and viewpoints of all affected project stakeholders (not just the data modeler). The project team needs to feel that it has an ownership stake in the model.

- The model should be used to drive discussion of the project requirements, and agreement about the work to be done.

- The model should capture only the necessary amount of information needed to achieve a specific purpose.

- Development of the model should continually move the project effort forward to a successful completion.

- The model should deliver maximum value for the stakeholder investment.

Models that are both MDD models and Agile models are *not* BDUF (Big Design Up Front)! They capture important project requirements, facilitate discussion and agreement about how these requirements will be met, capture and document the nature of the agreement(s), and help drive the subsequent design and implementation of the solution. They are also used post-production to support and maintain the solution.

PRINCIPLES OF AGILE DATA MODELING

As described in the previous section, data modeling should be an *interactive* process involving all concerned and knowledgeable stakeholders. Note: this will not be the entire project team, usually just business stakeholders, subject-matter experts (SMEs), and system/application architects. It should also be an iterative process, wherein the model is gradually fleshed out over time as user stories are elaborated and project requirements become better understood.

When data modeling becomes an interactive, group activity, then the data model becomes the property of the team (not just the data modeler), and the team has an ownership interest in the model. Although this shifting away of ownership from the data modeler to the team may make data modelers apprehensive, it's important that the project team feel this sense of ownership. Otherwise, they will regard the model as nothing more than someone else's attempt at documenting requirements, and they will not trust the data model or use it throughout the project. Therefore, it will have little or no value to the project and will not contribute materially to the project's success. Also, as previously noted, a data model should tell both a *true story* (that is, it should accurately reflect the current state of the business) and a *good story* (that is, it should provide a path forward to a *better* future state of the business). Here are some other useful principles of Agile data modeling:

- We can/should model as much as we know (or think we know) of the requirements at any given point in time. It is OK to model somewhat in advance of the user stories if doing so will help drive useful conversations about them.

- Confine the logical data model to business data requirements, definitions, rules, and constraints. Put any application-specific data requirements in the physical design.

- Document all definitions, assumptions, business rules, decisions, and agreements. As mentioned previously, it's also a good idea to capture the association between user stories and entities/attributes.

- Use the data model to drive conversations around the user stories and how the functional requirements of the project will be implemented. I've found data models to be extremely useful during user story elaborations, user story analysis, and design, and the creation of user story test cases.

- Use data model design patterns where possible (but take care to ensure that they are appropriate).

Keeping the logical data model business-focused, application-independent, and Agile is the best way to ensure its acceptance and use by an Agile project team!

Key Points

- A logical data model is the business requirements view of data, defined at the business subject area or higher. It contains business data definitions, rules, relationships, and constraints for an area of the business.

- A logical data model should be independent of any specific application, implementation, or usage of the data.

- A logical data model changes only in response to changes in business data requirements (or our understanding of them).

- Decoupling the logical data model from specific applications and database implementations is the key to making data models Agile and supporting the business's need for data that is not tightly coupled to specific applications.

- A logical data model should be both an MDD model and an Agile model. It should be owned and updated (interactively and incrementally) by the project team (under the guidance and direction of the data modeler), and used to capture and model business data requirements, drive discussions and agreements, direct the design and generate at least part of the solution.

- A data model should tell both a *true story* (that is, it should accurately reflect the current state of the business) and a *good story* (that is, it should provide a path forward to a *better* future state of the business).

- Keeping the logical data model business-focused, application-independent, and Agile is the best way to ensure its acceptance and use by an Agile project team.

Chapter 12
Agile Database Design

Database schemas are notoriously volatile, extremely concrete, and highly depended on. This is one reason why the interface between OO applications and databases is so difficult to manage, and why schema updates are generally painful.

Robert C. Martin

In the previous chapter, we noted the importance of decoupling the logical data model (i.e., the business data requirements) from the physical instantiation of the data itself (e.g., the physical database design). This decoupling gives us the ability to do our data modeling in a more Agile fashion in response to new user stories and changing business requirements.

Now we need to look at how to do physical data (or database) design in an Agile manner, especially regarding decoupling the physical instantiation of the data from application consumption.

WHAT IS PHYSICAL DATA DESIGN?

A physical data design can be defined as *the mapping of some subset of the logical data model to an appropriate choice of architecture and technology.* As mentioned before, the logical data model doesn't dictate how (or whether) any given entity or attribute will be physically instantiated. Many people assume that every logical model will be instantiated as a relational database, but this is not necessarily the case. I have implemented data models as XML and JSON schema definitions for example, and dimensional data structures for BI and reporting. I've jokingly said that it's entirely possible to implement a given data model as an office filing cabinet![76]

A physical data design supports one or more applications or uses of data, out of the number of possible applications or uses that a logical data model can support within a given business subject area.

This instantiation of data does not (necessarily) need to be a database, it does not (necessarily) have to be relational, and it does not (necessarily) need to be normalized. These are design choices dictated by the requirements of the application. A multi-user transactional application will benefit more from a more normalized relational database schema; an online catalog will probably need to use a document repository, and a BI application may need a dimensional (fact/dimension) database.

GOALS OF PHYSICAL DATA DESIGN

A good physical data design tries to accomplish the following goals[77]:

- The design should be *highly cohesive;* That is, it should put associated data in one place for easy accessibility. Applications should get to the data they need quickly and easily, ideally with a single call.

---

[76] John Giles points out that, for some applications such as missile guidance systems, the data exists entirely in memory. Nonetheless, one can safely assume that there's a data (or class) model defining the structure of the data even if it never gets beyond memory.

[77] I go into much more detail on physical data and database design in my book *Building the Agile Database* (Technics Publications LLC, 2011).

- The design should also be *loosely coupled* (i.e., robust and non-volatile). A change to one data component should not break applications using other data components. For example, you want to avoid a situation where a schema change to a single table causes multiple services to fail.

- Ideally, the physical data design should be *reusable*. That is, able to support multiple applications and multiple uses of the data. For example, I did a post-mortem on a failed project where a database was created to support software programming for an engine component. The database design was so constrained that it could not be used to support programming for any other sort of engine component, or even for any other version of the one component it was designed to support! We redesigned the database to support the programming of multiple versions of multiple engine components. We then had to do a (very slight) additional redesign when programming for vehicle components was offered as well.

- The physical data design should be *well-performing*, both for updates and for queries.

- Most importantly, the physical data design should be *consistent with business data rules and definitions*. The First Rule of physical data design is this: Never allow the persistence or representation of data to violate the business' understanding of the business data!

I use the acronym PRISM to represent the five principles of good physical data design:

- *Performance and Ease of Use*. Quick and easy access to data by approved users in a usable and business-relevant form so as to maximize the business value of both applications and data.

- *Reusability*. Design data persistence and delivery to support multiple applications and uses of data within a business subject area to increase ROI and business value.

- *Integrity*. Ensure that data always has a valid business meaning and value, regardless of context, and that the data always reflects a valid state of the business.

- *Security*. Ensure that data is available only to authorized persons and that only those with the designated authority to update business data can do so.

- *Maintainability*. Deliver data *at a cost that yields value*; that is, ensure that the cost of creating, using, maintaining, and disposing of data does not exceed its value to the business.

COHESION AND COUPLING

A good physical data design takes into account the object-oriented concepts of *Cohesion* and *Coupling*. Without getting too deeply into the theory, a good data design tries to accomplish the following things:

- Changes in applications should not break data structures.
- Changes in data structures should not break applications.
- Data structures should be able to support multiple applications.
- Data structures should be quickly and easily updateable.
- Applications should be able to get data quickly and easily from one place.

But, as you've probably noticed, some of these goals appear to be mutually exclusive! Non-normalized data structures support cohesion but result in tight-coupling and inability to support reuse. Every application has to get the same data from the same place, and a change to a single data structure can break multiple applications. Also, since everybody is getting their data from the same place, it can result in locking and blocking in the database and subsequent performance issues for applications. Normalized data structures reduce coupling, increase data reusability and performance and help ensure data quality but make data less cohesive. Applications must do multiple calls to multiple data structures to create a coherent set of data for their users.

This condition is sometimes referred to as the *Object/Relational Impedance Mismatch*,[78] and is one of the biggest problems in Agile data design. How can we provide applications with easy-to-access cohesive sets of data while ensuring data robustness, data quality, and good performance?

ABSTRACTION AND ENCAPSULATION

The answer is to call upon two more object-oriented concepts: *Abstraction* and *Encapsulation*. Abstraction means identifying the critical functionality that needs to be made available to the user (i.e., the "What"). Encapsulation means packaging this functionality in a way that hides the manner of the implementation (i.e., the "How) from the user. The idea is to present an easy-to-use interface that enables the "What" while hiding the "How". You don't have to know anything about electricity to turn on a light switch or know anything about mechanics to operate a car.

In physical data design, one way of using abstraction and encapsulation to overcome cohesion and coupling problems is to use *data virtualization*, which I refer to in *Building the Agile Database* as the Virtual Data Layer, or VDL. Instead of allowing applications to access data structures directly, we impose a layer of abstraction between the application layer and the data persistence layer (see Figure 4). In relational databases, this abstraction can take the form of views (including materialized views for DBMSs that support them), table-valued

---

[78] This is actually a misnomer; the condition should more properly be called the *Cohesion/Coupling Impedance Mismatch*. It really doesn't have anything to do with relational databases at all.

functions, user-defined datatypes, and stored procedures or stored functions. There is also third-party data virtualization software available (e.g., Cisco's Composite and Denodo). Using services, including microservices, is another good way to abstract the consumption and updating of data.[79]

Application	User Interface
	Business Layer
	App. Data Layer
Database	DB Virtual Data Layer (VDL)
	Database Schema
	DB Physical Design
Requirements	Logical Data Model
	Conceptual Data Model
	Business Data Requirements

Figure 4: The Data Services Stack

Data virtualization confers several advantages for applications that use and update data. The data abstraction layer can pull together data from multiple sources quickly and efficiently and present them to applications as a single set of data; applications do not need to figure out how to do the necessary joins, and the data layer can do this work faster and more efficiently than the application.

---

[79] Some people would also include object-relational mappings, such as Microsoft's Entity Framework, in this list. However, I believe there is still a risk in coupling application object classes directly to tables in the database schema, and advise against this. When using O/R frameworks, I believe in reading data from a view, and updating data via stored procedures attached to the object class.

This gives applications a cohesive view of data. At the same time, using application-specific views or services make it less likely that a given change to the database schema will break multiple applications or application services. And keeping the database design independent of any specific application increases the chance of data reuse to support multiple applications and services.

One last important physical design principle: keep the work of data persistence and delivery on the database server as much as possible (or on the data virtualization server). Overloading the application server with filtering, sorting, integrating, and reformatting data can create performance bottlenecks, overload networks, and reduce the scalability of applications. I'm a firm believer in "letting the database do the data work", and returning to the application only the data it needs, rather than sending all the data in the database to the application for processing.[80]

PRINCIPLES OF AGILE DATA DESIGN

To accommodate an Agile approach to doing physical data design and database implementation on projects, keep the following principles in mind:

- Implement only as much as you need to support the active user stories. Refactoring data structures and objects after they've been created can be expensive and time-consuming, so do this only when you must. You can also implement minor entities (i.e., code tables) and, when necessary, parent entities to support foreign key (FK) constraints. However, do not implement non-key attributes for these parent tables until user stories exist that need them.

- Have a clear understanding of both the logical (business) and physical (application) data requirements. Create a physical design that maps

---

[80] See the section entitled "In Defense of the Intelligent Database" in my book *Building the Agile Database*, pp. 81-84.

the logical to the physical in a way that satisfies application requirements without persisting the data in ways that violate business data definitions, rules, and constraints.

- Buffer the data (or database) schema with virtual objects to insulate the application from changes in the underlying schema.

- Model what you know; implement only what you need.

- Automate the process of generating database schemas and objects as much as possible. We generate database schemas and objects directly from our data models, using the macro capabilities of our modeling tool, and we auto-generate database update stored procedures (aka, "CRUD" procedures) directly from the database schema, with no hand-coding.

- When refactoring, refactor as early as possible (before too much code is written), and refactor at as high a level as possible (e.g., try to refactor in views rather than at the schema level).

- Refactor in a way that minimizes the impact to applications and to project resources and timelines. Each refactoring should result in forward progress.

By keeping both Agile and Object-Oriented principles in mind, designing according to the PRISM principles, making judicious use of data virtualization, and keeping data work on the database server, you can create data structures that are robust, performant, easy to refactor and maintain, and value-producing.

Key Points

- A physical data design can be defined as the mapping of some subset of the logical data model to an appropriate choice of architecture and technology.

- A physical data design supports one or more applications or uses of data, out of the number of possible applications or uses that a logical data model can support within a given business subject area.

- The instantiation of data does not (necessarily) need to be a database, it does not (necessarily) have to be relational, and it does not (necessarily) need to be normalized. These are design choices that are dictated by the requirements of the application.

- Physical data and database structures should be highly-cohesive, loosely-coupled, reusable, and performant. They should persist and represent data in ways that do not violate business data definitions, rules, and constraints.

- The acronym PRISM reminds us that data structures should be **P**erformant, **R**eusable, guarantee data **I**ntegrity and **S**ecurity, and be easy to **M**aintain.

- Use the object-oriented principles of abstraction and encapsulation (i.e., data virtualization) to solve the design problems of cohesion and coupling.

- Use abstract data objects to decouple and insulate applications from the impact of changes to the underlying database schema.

- To the greatest extent possible, keep data "heavy lifting" on the database (or data virtualization) server, and return to the application only the data it needs.

Chapter 13
Agile BI and Analytics

The greatest value of a picture is when it forces us to notice what we never expected to see.

John W. Tukey

So far, we've covered the Agile implications of architecture, logical data design, and physical data design. To conclude, let me say a few words about the Agile consumption of data for BI (Business Intelligence) and analytics applications.[81]

THE BI PROBLEM

When our IT department made me the BI Architect as well as the data architect, I was confronted with an immediate problem: our IT department had never made any provision for BI and analytics! We didn't, for example, have anything remotely resembling a data warehouse, or a Master Data Management (MDM) Repository. We didn't have a data governance or DQM (Data Quality Management) organization. In short, we didn't have any way of creating,

---

[81] See my book, *Growing Business Intelligence* (Technics Publications, 2016) for a more in-depth examination of this topic.

managing, or publishing canonical data across our organization. All organizational reporting and analytics was done from transactional databases, which introduced the risks of inconsistent data definitions and poor data quality. We tried to mitigate these risks in the following ways:

- We started doing business subject-area data modeling (i.e., defining data in a consistent way across multiple applications within a business domain).

- We used these data models to generate the schemas for application databases according to a defined set of database design standards.

- Data value constraints (e.g., primary key, foreign key, alternate key, domain, and check constraints) were defined and implemented in the database schema rather than enforced by applications.

- Applications were required to use Fundamental Stored Procedures (aka, "CRUD" procedures) to update database structures. These auto-generated FSPs use a template that ensures transactional consistency across multiple stored procedure calls, provides for "optimistic updating" (which allows multiple users to update the same table, but not the same record), and provides immediate feedback to the application if a database error occurs.

These database design standards and practices served two primary purposes: they enabled business users to do reporting and analytics from transactional data with a minimum of heartburn, and they enabled a small handful of DBAs to successfully manage and support thousands of application databases.

Even after our organization created a data lake in the cloud, it consisted of transactional data forklifted from application databases and moved as-is into the cloud, with views created (occasionally) over the data to facilitate reporting. We still had no repository for canonical or master data or any process for creating, managing, and publishing it.

THE BI PATTERN APPROACH

Eventually, we got authorization and funding to purchase both an MDM repository and a Data Quality Management (DQM) tool (but *not* a data warehouse, which would have taken too long and cost too much money). It was left to me to figure out how to get us from where we were currently to a more acceptable future state for BI and analytics. This is a case in which an Agile approach is mandated; we had to support current organizational reporting and analytics needs while "working toward" a more desirable solution.

To do this, I came up with a pattern-based approach, as follows:

- *Pattern 1 – Quick Wins*. Before we had a data lake in the cloud, we had to do reporting and BI from on-prem transactional databases. To protect transactional applications from the performance impacts of ad-hoc user reporting access, we created read-only replications of our transactional databases on other servers and put reporting views on them to help insulate reporting applications from the impact of database schema changes (see Figure 5a on page 155). Local data (such as spreadsheets) could be uploaded directly to the visualization (reporting) server.[82]

- *Pattern 2 – Forklift*. When the cloud became available to us, we used a data replication tool to move our data directly from transactional databases to a data lake, reducing the need for replicated databases (some of our applications were moved to the replicated databases if they didn't need to update data, to reduce the load on the servers hosting transactional applications). We defined a cloud database for "raw" data, in which the data was defined exactly the same way as in the source database, with no data cleansing or reformatting. To make the data easier (and safer) to consume, we created reporting views over this data and encouraged our

---

[82] Most of our business users are using Tableau for reporting and visualization. Our BI Center of Excellence uses mostly Python.

business users to connect their reporting tools to these views rather than to the underlying data schemas (see Figure 5b on page 156).

- One of our divisions implemented this pattern using a data appliance, in which the data is stored on the appliance server in a denormalized, proprietary format and then accessed through information views defined on that server.

- In the absence of an MDM repository, we extracted metadata from our data modeling tool and moved it to the BI database so that business users could have access to data definitions, formats, domains, etc.

- *Pattern 3 – DQM.* Once a Data Quality Management (DQM) tool became available, we created a second cloud database in our data lake for cleansed data (we refer to this as the "Staged" database). Data quality constraints are defined in the DQM tool, and data from the "raw" database is processed through the tool and moved to the "staged" database. Again, reporting views are used to insulate the reporting/visualization tools from the impact of the data shift (see Figure 5c on page 156).

Once data is moved to the "staged" database, business users must do reporting from that database; they will no longer have access to the "raw" database. Only IT people in the BI Center of Excellence (i.e., data scientists) will have access to the "raw" database.

- *Pattern 4 – MDM.* With an MDM repository now in our toolkit, we can begin work on two essential components of data management: creating and managing a source of canonical data that can be used across the organization and creating ways of publishing this data to our applications (see Figure 5d on page 157).

- Canonical data can be updated automatically from the data in the "Cleansed" data repository and managed directly by authorized business users as part of a data governance process. Data in the MDM repository can be published directly to application databases (and the data visualization server) via scheduled batch processes and/or made available to services via APIs.

- *Pattern 5 – Streaming Analytics.* As more of our products become part of the "Internet of Things", we need to decide what to do with the vast amounts of streaming data coming into our organization. We also need to find a way to leverage the results of the data analyses coming out of our Data Analytics Center of Excellence. In *Growing Business Intelligence*, I proposed a "Symbiotic Model" that mines streaming and analytics data to produce canonical data, which is moved into the MDM Repository.[83] This data is then used to inform subsequent data analyses, and so on (see Figure 5e on page 157). In other words, we use canonical data to turn raw/streaming/unstructured data into more canonical data, which better informs our subsequent data analytics.

PRINCIPLES OF AGILE BI

Please note that the patterns described above are not prescriptive; that is, you can use other patterns and sequences of patterns.[84] The important concept here is using a Pattern-based approach to incrementally get your organization from its

---

[83] *Growing Business Intelligence*, pp. 66-67. Prior to 2019, we were using an on-prem Operational Data Store (ODS) as our "Data Lake", and were looking at migrating to Hadoop to better accommodate our streaming data. By 2019, we had decided to move everything to the Cloud, and deprecate our on-prem ODS. Also, we had created several dimensional data marts on our ODS platform, but decided to move those to the cloud as well. Again, it's important to be able to pivot your Data and BI solutions quickly, as new technologies become available.

[84] As noted above, we have pivoted away from an ODS to a data lake, abandoned the idea of a data warehouse, and are currently deprecating the use of dimensional data marts.

current state of data management, data governance, data quality management, and BI/data analytics to a more value-producing future state. You will not be able to do everything all at once, so prioritize your organization's needs and strengths and choose your patterns appropriately.

To accommodate an Agile approach to data management and BI, keep the following principles in mind:

- Tie BI initiatives to specific business outcomes. Measure the business value of each step in your BI/analytics journey, and publicize it throughout the organization to gain support for the next step.

- Deliver BI value continuously and incrementally. The business needs to see that their money is yielding results.

- Focus on data transparency rather than data quality. Use metadata to answer questions about the source, currency, business meaning, transformations and cleansing, etc., so that business users can make intelligent choices about how much to trust the data for any given business usage.

- Decouple information delivery from data storage using views or other sorts of data virtualization. Store data in an information-neutral state (i.e., as data, not as information). Allow the business to define data meaning and implement data delivery in an easily modified form as business meanings and information needs change.

- Focus on data in motion, not data at rest. In other words, the end goal is not to create a static repository of data; the end goal is to be continually delivering trusted data to people who need it. BI initiatives tend to focus on the data repository rather than the data delivery—it needs to be the other way around!

- Have a strategy for identifying and mitigating risks throughout the process. Mitigate the most crucial risks at the beginning of each project.

- Take an Agile approach to data governance. Use a "non-invasive" approach to ensure that the business always has access to the data it needs to operate, and remove IT bottlenecks to data. At the same time, create "feedback loops" to inform the business of potential data problems in a timely manner.[85]

- Automate the delivery of data as much as possible, using tools and processes that minimize the amount of effort required.

- Use trusted data to make your organization more "data-driven" and less dependent on "gut instinct" decision-making.

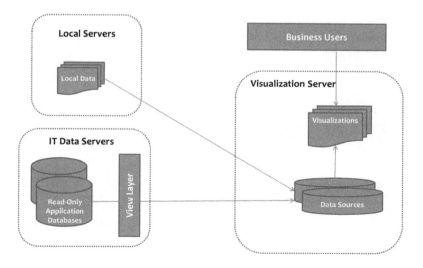

Figure 5a: Pattern 1 – Quick Wins

---

[85] For one project, we wrote a process that used regex validation to identify problems in a data store. The problems were logged in a database table, which was connected to an online report that the users could look at each morning.

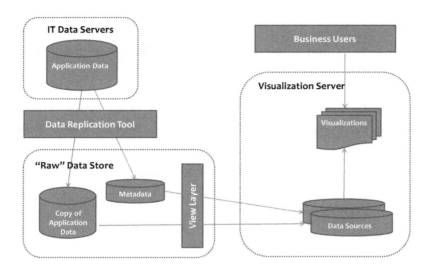

Figure 5b: Pattern 2 – Forklift

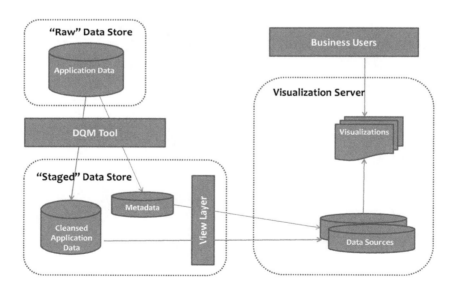

Figure 5c: Pattern 3 – DQM

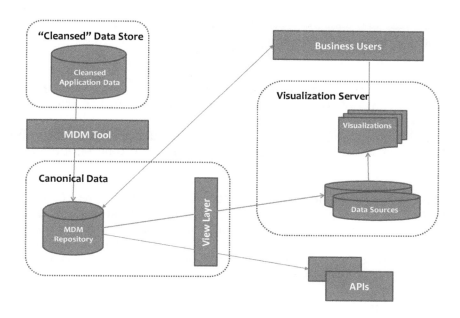

Figure 5d: Pattern 4 – MDM

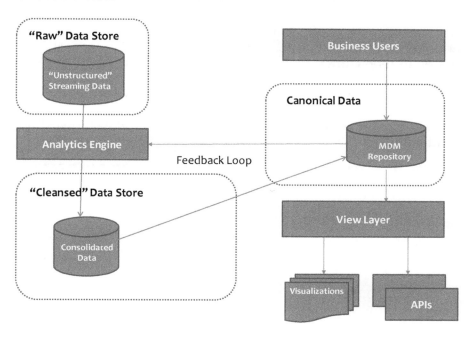

Figure 5e: Pattern 5 – Streaming Analytics

Key Points

- Use an incremental, pattern-based approach to get your organization from its current data/BI state to a more acceptable future state.

- At each state, make sure you deliver measurable business value and publicize that value throughout the organization to gain support for future initiatives.

- Persist data in an information-neutral state (i.e., as data, not as information). Decouple the delivery of data from its storage and allow the business to control the information meaning of data.

- As much as possible, try to streamline data and BI delivery in a way that eliminates IT bottlenecks and puts the business in control.

- Focus on data transparency rather than data quality. Deliver higher-quality data in successive iterations, but use metadata to answer business' questions about the trustworthiness of the data.

- Focus on data in motion, not data at rest. Ensure that data and information are delivered on time to people who need it, not just persisted in repositories.

- Keep data governance Agile, business-focused, and non-invasive.

- Use trusted data to make your organization more "data-driven" and less dependent on "gut instinct" decision-making.

Section III
The Challenging Landscape

Creativity thrives on a constant diet of challenges and opportunities, which are often one and the same.

Lee Clow

Our data modeling and data management work does not take place in a vacuum. As mentioned in the previous section, our work takes place in a context that includes *Technology*, *People*, *Business*, and *Data*. On every project, we must adapt our activities to stakeholders, methodologies, business requirements, technology constraints, and the type(s) of data within our scope.

Since I started doing data and database work on Agile projects more than 15 years ago, I've had to adapt my work to any number of context-related changes:

- *People*. When I started out, I was working entirely with in-house staff, most of whom had been with our company for decades. All were extremely knowledgeable about the company and its business, and all were excellent at their respective jobs. In those days, we taught classes on data modeling, database design, and SQL coding, and made sure that everyone understood our standards and best practices and the reasons for them. This made it a lot easier to work with developers, analysts, and testers on projects.

Now, most of the people I work with on projects are contractors, and many of them work overseas. They don't know anything about our business, standards, or our data. Since there is a constant turnover of contract staff, there's no time (or bandwidth) to train them, and it's a real effort to keep everybody informed of what we expect from them and why. Most colleges and universities don't teach data management, and a lot of the contractors I work with are not very conversant with database technology, data modeling, or SQL coding. This means I have to do a lot more teaching on projects and be careful not to make assumptions about what people should know. Language skills vary as well, making communication difficult sometimes.

- *Technology.* I started out working with client/server applications, all of which used relational databases. Then came XML-based web services, which decoupled both functionality from applications and data from databases. The client/server application architecture was replaced by MVC (Model-View-Controller), applications became collections of objects and object methods, and applications could use object (ORM) frameworks to abstract data and update databases. XML was supplanted by JSON, and relational databases got competition from both object databases and NoSQL databases like MongoDB. Web services running on on-prem EAI hubs are now moving to microservices in the Cloud. Cloud-based architecture means less emphasis on performance tuning and scalability, both for applications and databases. There's a push to *domain-driven* application design, with significant implications for both data modeling and database design. And an emphasis on CI/CD (Continuous Integration and Continuous Deployment) means we have to do our work even faster than before and with significantly more automation.

- *Business*. Agile methodologies have brought the business front and center, which means that IT people need to be conversant with business processes, practices and vernacular, and be able to communicate effectively with business people. Agile also means that business people are less tolerant of IT bottlenecks and expect IT to deliver results quickly and with minimum fuss. We can no longer act like trolls working in caves.

- *Data*. When I started out, data was always designed to Third Normal Form[86], and implemented in relational databases in Third Normal Form. The idea that data could be persisted in other ways hadn't really occurred to anybody. Then came Ralph Kimball and dimensional data marts, followed by XML and JSON and document databases, object databases, and NoSQL databases. The notion of business-area data modeling is challenged by a new approach called *domain-driven design*. Subject-area databases that can support multiple applications are challenged by a *microservices-based* approach to application and database design. It seems that we are taking steps backward to the "bad old days" of application-specific data persistence silos – this raises the question: where will canonical data come from?

So it makes sense, at this point, to take a look at some of these challenges and see how we might be able to respond to them, in an Agile fashion, without completely sacrificing all of our fundamental data management principles.

---

[86] Or whatever the appropriate degree of normalization was for that model.

Chapter 14
Schema-less Databases

NoSQL databases emerged from unmet needs.

Dan Sullivan, "NoSQL for Mere Mortals"

One argument I hear more and more against data modeling is that data modeling pertains only to relational databases and a "table-based" view of data. Now that we have non-relational databases, we no longer need to define a schema in advance of data creation and hence no longer need data models. But is this true? Is the only purpose of a data model to pre-define a schema for a database? (You should already know the answer to this by now!) Let's explore this subject a bit further.

CHARACTERISTICS OF SCHEMA-LESS DATABASES

Schema-less databases (also called "NoSQL" databases, or "Schema On Read" databases) differ from relational-type databases in the following ways:

- You don't have to predefine a schema before loading data into the database. NoSQL databases will accept and store any data sent to them, in any format, under any name. Data is structured and organized when it is extracted from the database via query and sent to the requestor (hence, "schema on read" rather than "schema on write").

- Furthermore, in NoSQL databases, data definitions are not fixed. The definition of the data can be changed from one record to the next!

- NoSQL databases store data as documents in hierarchical form rather than as tables.[87]

- Relationships are expressed hierarchically rather than as primary key/foreign key associations.[88]

- A NoSQL database can be spread across multiple servers (called horizontal scaling), rather than being confined to a single physical server. This gives NoSQL databases the ability to quickly scale out to store very large amounts of data very inexpensively.

- Business data rules are generally not enforced in NoSQL databases— these rules must be encoded in an application.[89] NoSQL databases are designed for performance and scalability, not for data integrity.

- Data can be duplicated throughout the database, in different documents, and in multiple hierarchy levels of the same document.[90]

---

[87] Other types of NoSQL databases store data as key-value pairs or graphs (nodes and links).

[88] Although documents can reference other documents directly.

[89] A good idea is to encode all the business data rules for a given NoSQL database in a stand-alone application and run it periodically against the database, sending alerts to business users if data anomalies are found. This way, you don't have to code the business rules into every application that runs against the database, and risk having the rules coded differently in different applications.

[90] For this reason, it is a good idea to create a set of what I call "canonical queries", queries that return the canonical values for a specified set of data. For example, if Product names and descriptions occur in multiple

- SQL databases enforce integrity of data updates (what are referred to as ACID properties: Atomicity, Consistency, Isolation, Durability). Transactional updates are immediately applied to the database upon commit. NoSQL databases don't support transactional updating; rather, they support "eventual consistency" of the data across multiple servers.[91]

So how do we do data modeling for NoSQL databases? First of all, it depends on the reason for using NoSQL. If we are using NoSQL because we have no idea what the structure of the data is, but we need to persist it so that we can explore and understand it (for example, data profiling of unstructured content from a search of Internet websites), then modeling of the data will be done after the fact, as the properties and characteristics of the data are analyzed, understood, and documented. In this case, the data model becomes an artifact of the data profiling process, used to communicate the profiling results to stakeholders.

If NoSQL is being used to persist data whose structure and properties are known and understood (for reasons of performance, scalability and/or cost), then data modeling can – and should – be done in advance of database creation, as would be done with any relational database.

Why? Precisely because a NoSQL database will accept any data thrown at it, under any name, and in any location in a document hierarchy, and because the format of a document can change from one record to the next! As Ryan Smith, Information Architect at Nike, says in his Introduction to Steve Hoberman's book,[92] "MongoDB would not hesitate to allow you to sequentially save four records in the same collection with field names of zipCode, zipcode, ZipCode

---

places in the database, there should be a query that returns the canonical list of Product names and descriptions.

[91] This is referred to as BASE: Basically Available, Soft-State, Eventual Consistency.

[92] *Data Modeling for MongoDB*, op. cit., pp. v-vi.

and postalCode, respectively. Each of these variations will be treated as a new field, with no warnings given. Everything will work great until you ask for your zipCode values back, and only one document out of four has a field by that name."

Actually, it's even worse than that because NoSQL databases don't enforce strong data typing. MongoDB would also let you put data values such as "N/A", "January 4th, 2010", 'EA-1B-23-C4-DF-9A', and -48392489.56 in any of your zip code or postal code fields, making it even more problematic when a business user tries to query regional sales figures by zip code. Not to mention that any user trying to query this data needs to know what database, collection, and document to look in and what level of the document hierarchy to query.

In other words, it is more difficult (and thus, more important) in NoSQL databases to organize and persist data in a way that enables end-users to retrieve data easily, with confidence in the results. A good data model is essential to making sure that everybody knows and agrees with how and where the data will be stored and under what name. To quote Ryan Smith again: "The flexible schema is a great innovation for quick evolution of your data model, and yet it requires discipline to harvest the benefits without experiencing major data quality issues and other frustrations as a result."

DATA MODELING FOR SCHEMA-LESS DATABASES

As explained previously, it is always possible to do logical data modeling of any data landscape, even when the target DBMS is non-relational. Take, for example, the following data model (which I created in my E-R modeling tool):

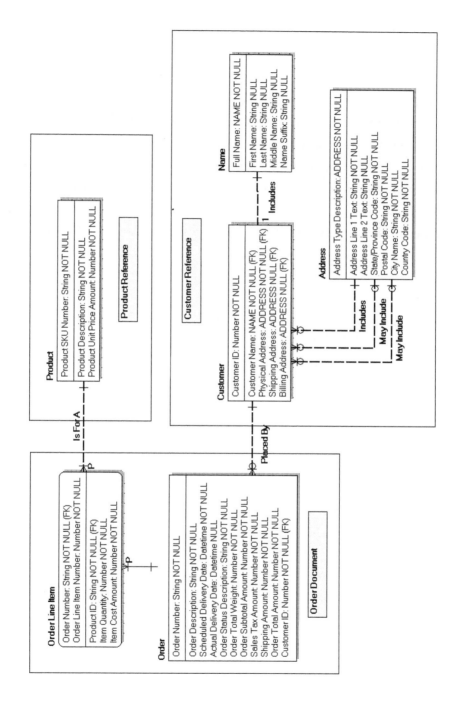

This data model shows three documents pertaining to a customer order. Two of the documents are reference documents. In other words, this company does both customer and product MDM. Customer and product data are overseen by one or more master data management groups, and the mastered datasets are published into the order database. The order document references a customer master record and contains embedded order line items, each referencing a product master record. Each customer document embeds a customer name (containing first, last and middle names, and an optional suffix) and one or more customer addresses (the physical address is mandatory in this model; the shipping and billing addresses are optional). An instance of a customer order might look something like this:

```
{
 Customer :
  {
 CustomerID : 1752341
 CustomerName :
  {
 CustomerFullName : "BurnsCo"
 CustomerFirstName : "Lawrence"
 CustomerLastName : "Burns"
 CustomerMiddleName : "E"
 CustomerSuffix :
  }
 PhysicalAddress :
  {
 AddressLine1Text : "2255 South Park Lane"
 AddressLine2Text : "Suite 101"
 CityName : "Foreston"
 StateCode : "WA"
 PostalCode : "98136"
 CountryCode: "USA"
  }
  }

 Product :
  {
 ProductID : "G75W37852-J1"
 ProductDescription : "Rotary Bivalve Inductor"
 ProductUnitPriceAmount : 68.99
  }
 CustomerOrder :
  {
 OrderNumber : "A9107Z4N54"
 OrderDescription : "Order From BurnsCo Dated 12/29/2018"
```

```
ScheduledDeliveryDate : ISODate("2019-01-15")
ActualDeliveryDate :
OrderStatusDescription : "Order Placed"
OrderTotalWeight : 22.5
OrderSubtotalAmount : 137.98
SalesTaxAmount : 13.45
ShippingAmount : 22.50
OrderTotalAmount : 173.93
CustomerID : 1752341
Order Line Item :
{
LineItemNumber : 1
ProductID : "G75W37852-J1"
ItemQuantity : 2
ItemCostAmount : 137.98
}
}
}
```

Note that the data model serves multiple purposes here: it presents the data landscape of a customer order in very easy-to-understand terms; it denotes the names and datatypes of the documents (entities) and their attributes; it describes the relationships between the various embedded and reference documents. The data model clarifies that customer and product need to be implemented as reference documents related to the customer order document via keys, while order line items are embedded within the customer order document itself.

PHYSICAL DESIGN FOR SCHEMA-LESS DATABASES

Physical design in NoSQL databases such as MongoDB is much more complex, and requires more forethought.[93] For one thing, it is necessary to decide whether 1-N relationships between documents (entities) should be handled via embedding or via reference. To decide, it's important to understand both the cardinality of relationships (which can be done in the logical model) and the requirements (if any) for referencing documents as stand-alone entities. If the cardinality is fairly low ("one-to-few") and you don't need to access the sub-

---

[93] An excellent explanation of some basic concepts of physical design in MongoDB can be found in a series of articles by William Zola at the following link: https://bit.ly/3xlMfjm.

documents outside the context of the parent document, you may embed. However, if the cardinality is "one-to-many" or you need to access the child documents as stand-alone entities, you may reference the child documents inside the parent document (using an array). And if the cardinality is very high ("one-to-squillions"), you would use parent referencing (putting a reference to the parent document inside each child document).

You can also denormalize documents by, for instance, duplicating data from child documents inside of parent documents (using arrays). But this requires an understanding of the probable ratio of document reads to document updates. If the document is read much more often than it is updated, then the performance benefits of this sort of denormalization will outweigh the additional cost and complexity of multiple updates (assuming you're willing to run the risk of data anomalies in your database!). It is also necessary to ensure that adequate indexes exist for the most frequently anticipated database queries.

There are not, as far as I'm aware, any good tools for doing this sort of logical-to-physical transformation for NoSQL databases, or for directly generating a database schema definition (DDL) from a physical model, as is done with relational databases. This makes supporting Agile and DevOps projects using NoSQL databases more difficult, as model-driven development cannot be used.

Key Points

- Data modeling is important for NoSQL databases to ensure that everyone is on the same page about how a given piece of data is named, how it is defined, how it is typed, and where it is located in the document hierarchy.

- If the same piece of data may exist in multiple locations, we need to know which document contains the canonical value (for reporting purposes).

- We also need to know whether a given document will be embedded inside another document or exist outside as a reference document.

- In NoSQL databases, business data rules and constraints must usually be enforced by coding them in an external program, then run against the database multiple times a day to report any invalid data values.

- A set of canonical queries should also be developed to extract canonical datasets from the database for reporting purposes.

- It is difficult to do model-driven development for NoSQL databases since data modeling tools don't natively support these databases.

Chapter 15
Domain-Driven Development

Everything should be built top-down, except the first time. Simplicity does not precede complexity, but follows it.

Alan Perlis

A fairly recent development in application (and database) architecture is something called Domain-Driven Development (or *DDD* for short). In Domain-Driven Development, databases do not integrate applications or even application functions. Instead, the size and scope of databases are reduced to being little more than persistence containers for specific application functions or services. Talk about "Back to the Future"! But if this is, in fact, the future of application development, how can we, as data practitioners, respond effectively?

How Domain-Driven Development Works

Here, for example, is a traditional database linking two different applications[94]:

---

[94] From Sokhan, Berke. "Domain-Driven Design for Services Architecture". ThoughtWorks, August 17, 2015. https://thght.works/3xnHANB.

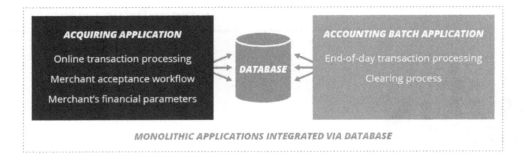

The applications are re-architected to communicate via messaging (service calls), and the database is broken up into separate databases for each application:

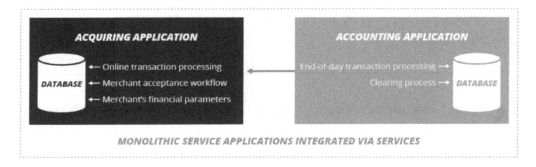

But even this is too much "tight coupling", as it combines multiple types of business processes within a single application. So the application is broken up into sub-domains, each of which has its own persistence store and each of which communicates via messaging:

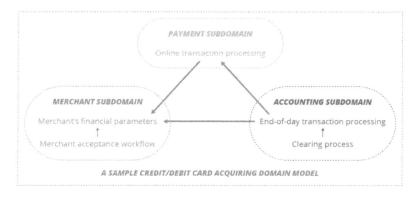

The primary reason for this choice of architecture is the speed of application development. By encapsulating both the application logic and the database schema within a particular sub-domain, each service can be developed and maintained by separate teams and deployed as often as the team wishes without having to consult or interact with other teams (e.g., the database team). It is further argued that this approach helps keep business logic from "leaking" into the database and replaces database transactions with application messaging.

A secondary argument for the domain-driven approach, according to Martin Fowler,[95] is that the business's understanding of the data (and the language it uses to express that understanding) varies from one domain to another. This is what makes it so difficult to create an enterprise-level data model, since, for example, the Sales Department's understanding of terms like Product and Customer may be different from that of, say, the Service Department.

Therefore, for the purposes of Domain-Driven Development, we can say that a "domain" represents an area of the business in which entities and attributes have the same meanings, and are similarly understood. A "subdomain" is a part of the domain supported by a common set of data and services.

DOMAIN-DRIVEN DEVELOPMENT AND DATA MODELING

This domain-driven approach to application development has several implications for data practitioners; let's examine them one by one:

1) First of all, this approach represents a real challenge for the data modeler. Instead of modeling for a single database, we will now have to model for multiple databases across multiple sub-domains while still trying to maintain common definitions for data that is used in multiple places. The solution for this is to create a *domain model*, which is essentially a business

---

[95] Fowler, Martin. "Bounded Context". January 15, 2014. https://martinfowler.com/bliki/BoundedContext.html.

subject-area model[96] with separate sub-models (or diagrams) for the various sub-domains. This ensures that data entities and attributes that are common across domains or sub-domains will at least be named and defined in the same way. It also ensures that intelligent questions will be asked about whether two similar entities or attributes are the same things or different things. We also need to know, for situations where the same entities or attributes exist in different databases, which of them contain the canonical values (i.e., the ones that should be used for organizational reporting and analytics).

This will necessitate almost constant communication with the various sub-domain development teams and their respective business subject-matter experts. Because of the challenge this presents (and because data modelers, as a general rule, prefer to model and implement data at as high a level as possible), the domain-driven approach has not found favor with most data professionals. However, as service-oriented application architecture (particularly the use of microservices) becomes more and more prevalent in our organizations, the domain-driven approach (and its attendant challenges) will almost certainly need to be addressed by data professionals. Without an over-arching domain model to keep data definitions consistent across multiple services, inconsistent data values will hamstring service messaging. Most developers recognize the importance of a domain-level data model, and we as data professionals must be ready and willing to meet this need. As Fowler notes[97]:

---

[96] My recommendation is to define the domain model at as high a level as is feasible, as close to a business subject model as is possible. This will enable Entity and Attribute definitions to be reused across the diagrams for the different sub-domains. Remember that a domain model encompasses an area of the business within which a given set of business terms have the same meaning.

[97] Fowler, Martin. "Multiple Canonical Models". July 21, 2003. https://bit.ly/3xf6WgA.

So far, however, it seems that the data modeling community is only beginning to catch on to this new world. This is sad because data modelers have a tremendous amount to offer to people building canonical messaging models.

2) There is a difference, as well as an overlap, between "Domain" in the business process sense and "Domain" in the Data sense. A data domain may support a related business process domain (e.g., Warranty Claim), or it may encompass multiple business process domains (e.g., Customer, Product).

3) Creating any "canonical model" for a business entity becomes much more challenging using this approach. Fowler notes[98] that a given sub-domain may implement only part of a canonical model (only the part that is needed to support service messaging). Also, this approach may result in what Fowler refers to as "multiple overlapping canonical models", no two of which may have the same structure (although, he says, there should be a translation between those parts of the models that overlap). In other words, two or more different domains may each have a product and/or customer representation, and those representations may differ because their definitions may differ across the different business areas. The following page contains an example from Martin Fowler.[99]

The challenge here for the data modeler is determining where these overlapping data entities are the same, and when they are different. In this example, Customer may mean exactly the same thing in both contexts (i.e., the person or company that purchases a product or service is the same person or company requiring support).

---

[98] Ibid.

[99] "Bounded Context", op. cit.

In this case, Customer becomes an entity in a canonical (or enterprise) data model, and gets reused for domains and subdomains that need it. But Product, in a Sales context, may actually mean something like Product Model, whereas Product, in a Service context, may be a specific *instance* of a Product Model. In this case, two entities (*Product* and *Product Model*) should be modeled instead of one. This demonstrates an important reason for data modeling in Domain-Driven Development: Without a data modeler to ask the right questions, we won't know whether the *Customer* and *Product* entities are the same things or different things. If they are the same thing (like *Customer*), then the entity and attribute definitions can be reused, ensuring consistency across the domain. If not, the different entities can now be properly named, defined, and understood.

4) In multiple overlapping canonical data structures split across multiple services (sub-domains), another issue surfaces, which Fowler refers to as

"N * N connections".[100] This occurs when, for example, services need to connect to and reference product and/or customer data stored within multiple other services. In this case, Fowler suggests, the multiply-referenced data should be extracted from the service databases and placed into a canonical data structure (database) in the hub of an Enterprise Service Bus (ESB).[101] This assumes, of course, that you have an ESB, and an ESB Hub, supporting your service-oriented architecture (SOA) environment. It also assumes that you are willing and able to do the work of refactoring both your applications (services) and databases. Note, however, that this puts you back in the position of integrating multiple applications/services through a database, which was exactly the "problem" you were trying to avoid in the first place!

5) This approach also leaves us with the problem of how to do organization-wide reporting and analytics, with the organization's data distributed across perhaps thousands of individual services. The only possible solution here is to periodically extract all of this data (or perhaps replicate it real-time via services) to a data warehouse. But again, this gets us right back to the problem we were trying to avoid in the first place: having to find a common "ubiquitous language" (i.e., ontology) to integrate data from multiple domains! It also assumes that an organization has a data warehouse or is willing to commit the time, money, and resources to create and maintain one. Again, without a domain-level data model to ensure consistency of data definitions (and identification of canonical data), populating a data warehouse from messaging stores would be impossible.

---

[100] "Multiple Canonical Models", op. cit.

[101] Or, as John Giles suggests, an operational data vault might be used for this purpose.

6) The issue of multiple, overlapping canonical data structures also brings us to the issue of Master Data Management (MDM). In these cases, it's a good bet that we have identified data that needs to be treated as master data. Master data should be maintained in an MDM repository of some sort, and either referenced from the repository via services or else published to a canonical data store of some sort (and referenced – not updated – by applications via services).

7) Martin Fowler asserts that these canonical data structures can be identified and built as-needed rather than planned up-front. However, there are two problems with what he refers to as the "harvesting" approach: the first is the amount of time and effort required for this refactoring, particularly if part of the refactoring involves MDM. The second problem, as I point out in *Building the Agile Database*, is that unless canonical data is properly modeled and implemented up-front, you may discover that it's not possible to refactor the data into a canonical model, as critical data values may be missing or invalid. I gave an example of this from my own experience earlier: the poorly-defined database for a time-reporting application needed to be refactored, but all the data had to be thrown out and re-entered because critical key data values were either missing or incorrect!

8) Regarding the desire of application developers to keep business logic out of the database, I agree that generally speaking, this is a good practice. However, it is (in my experience) often necessary to code application functions that require lots of heavy data lifting (sorting, filtering, etc.) in the database to ensure adequate application performance and scalability.[102] For example, in the Warranty application I'm currently working on, the code which needs to: a) identify all applicable warranties

---

[102] See my book *Building the Agile Database* for a more detailed exposition of this, particularly the section titled "In Defense of the Intelligent Database" (pp. 81-84).

for a particular product with certain characteristics and b) identify the applicable warranties for a particular type of product claim, had to be coded in the database instead of the application, to return the information to the user in an acceptable amount of time. Oftentimes, it is more efficient to use the resources of the database server, and the power of the DBMS's query optimizer, to do heavy data manipulation and return the results to the application, than it is to move perhaps millions of rows of data across the network to the application and perform the work there.

9) Lastly, I should point out that the domain-driven approach can generally only be used for applications that are developed in-house. Commercial off-the-shelf (COTS) products are nearly always monolithic applications that integrate several different business functions through a common database.

MODELING UP AND BUILDING DOWN

So, what we're faced with is a sort of paradox: good data management practices dictate that we try to model data at as high a level as possible, and empirical evidence suggests that we can only defer, not ignore, the issue of cross-domain ontologies (i.e., "ubiquitous language"). At the same time, software development practices are dictating the implementation of data at ever more granular levels.

My approach to dealing with this is what I call "Modeling Up and Building Down". In other words, while trying to deliver what developers need in a reasonable amount of time (within the confines of a sprint), I'm also trying to ask sufficient questions to determine whether the data requirements represent entities and attributes that are unique to a subdomain, are unique to a domain, or are canonical (that is, are more enterprise in nature, and span domains).

If my subdomain model needs an entity (say, Customer or Product Model) that is canonical, I will bring it in from my higher-level canonical or enterprise model, rather than remodeling it from scratch. If it needs an entity that has been (or can be) defined at a domain level (say, Warranty), I will model this at the domain level and then bring it into the subdomain. So I'm always modeling at as high a level as possible, and then I bring entities down into the subdomain model for implementation for a particular application or service (see Figure 8 on page 212).

This approach ensures that, even when the data itself is fragmented, the underlying data models are not so that data is at least consistently defined across the multiple data persistence stores.

My personal preference, though, has always been to design and build databases that can support multiple applications, services, and uses of data within a business domain, so as to get the maximum amount of value from both data and databases.

THE IMPORTANCE OF A CANONICAL DATA MODEL

When your application architecture includes services (SOA) or microservices, you have to face the fact that data may not be defined (or named) consistently in all places. For example, you may have an application web service that interfaces with a commercial ERP or CRM package, or another application in which similar data entities and attributes have different names or data formats.

In this case, it's handy to have a *Canonical Data Model (CDM)*. A CDM serves several useful purposes in a service-based application architecture. Principally, it acts as a translator, enabling, for example, a service from Application A to interact with data from Application B, which may have a different format and nomenclature than Application A's database. Remember the statement from Martin Fowler, above: When an application architecture contains "multiple overlapping canonical models", then some sort of translation service is required to act as an intermediary between them.

Here's an example[103]: In Figure 7a (page 188), we see four examples of address data formatted in several different ways (XML, CSV, and JSON), and in two different languages (English and Dutch). Assume that these four different representations of address are used in four different applications, and we want to connect these applications via web services. In our sample solution, we define a single canonical model for address, using XML Schema Definition (XSD). We'll do this in English since most Dutch people understand English, and few Americans understand Dutch. The canonical model appears in Figure 7b (page 189). Examples of XML data formatted according to the canonical model are shown in Figure 7c (page 189).

To communicate address data between applications, Application A would put its data into the canonical format, and send it via a service to Application B, which would put the data into its preferred format and store it. Application B could send address data to Application A using the same canonical format.[104]

Why do this? For one thing, using a canonical model reduces the number of translations required when multiple services connect multiple applications (i.e., Fowler's "N * N Connections" problem). Figure 7d (page 190) shows an example of this: without the CDM, 16 translations are required to connect six applications; with the CDM, only 12 translations are required. The number of translations required increases significantly as the number of applications being connected increases.

The second reason to use a CDM is to reduce translation maintenance when one of the applications is changed (perhaps to an entirely new application), and all of the service connections to that application need to change. In Figure 7e (page

---

[103] Taken from Paasschens, Emiel. "Benefits of a Canonical Data Model (CDM) in an SOA Environment". AMIS Technology Blog, August 8, 2016. https://bit.ly/35g1Rsy.

[104] I used canonical data models on a project involving Customer, Order, Product and Part data sent between several different applications, including ERP and CRM applications. These canonical models were used to create XML Schema Definitions (XSDs), which were then used to define data properties for the web services.

190), Application E has been removed and replaced with Application X. Without a CDM, there are eight translations that need to be changed (to and from each of four applications that interact with Application X). With a CDM, only two translations (between Application X and the CDM) need to be changed.

The third reason to use a CDM has to do with logic maintenance. If there is logic or orchestration that uses the data to determine where and how to route the message, and one of the connecting systems changes, then you need to check all logic to see if it uses some part of the data model of the connecting system; if so, the logic will have to be modified or rewritten. If a CDM is used, and the logic is written using the data model of the CDM, changes in applications will not require a rewrite of the logic, since that logic exists within the CDM (see Figure 7f on page 191). Otherwise, business logic associated with each connection (if any such exists) would have to be refactored.

In short, a CDM functions according to the Object-Oriented principles of Abstraction and Encapsulation that we talked about in the previous Chapter on physical data design. The CDM abstracts out the canonical data model and encapsulates any associated business logic or orchestration so that applications can more easily communicate with each other via services.

THE DANGER OF MODELING TOO SMALL

One very real danger of domain modeling is that, if you're not careful, you might model inconsistencies and contradictions in each business unit's view of the organization and its processes. This is why, as I pointed out above, it's important to have some sort of over-arching enterprise data model (or at least a Business Subject Area or canonical data model) that encompasses your various sub-domains.

Here's an example: for the Warranty application I'm currently working on, I first did a modeling session with the people who write Warranty Contracts. They walked me through the business process and the vernacular, and I created a first-draft Conceptual data model. Then I showed that model to the people who process Warranty Claims, and their response was "That's not the way our warranties work!" I had to bring both groups together and walk through the model; this conversation surfaced a number of previously undisclosed exception processes and differences in terminology that had to be worked into the model.

Had I modeled (and implemented) each of these sub-domains separately, the inconsistencies might not have become known until well into development, at which point the necessary refactoring would have been difficult, expensive, and painful.

In his book on data vault modeling, my good friend and colleague John Giles, emphasizes the importance of starting your modeling from some sort of enterprise-level ontology and/or universal data model pattern. This accomplishes two important purposes: first, it keeps the discussion of data requirements focused on the needs of the business; second, it helps the business resolve differences in perspective and vernacular that could otherwise impact the project. He gives as an example a data vault project with a customer "Hub" as one of the core concepts. The project floundered when consultants decided to create a "source-centric" (as opposed to "business-centric") data vault model around the separate views of customer in each application source system. This design allowed each source system's customer data set to be physically persisted more quickly, but the business still wasn't able to do anything remotely useful with the data (such as use it for organizational reporting or analytics around a central customer concept).

John Giles references some concepts from David Hay's book, *Achieving Buzzword Compliance.*[105] Hay recommends (1) the creation of a high-level, business-focused overview model, from which may emanate (2) multiple specific semantic models, each expressed in the language of separate business units. In this view, the

---

[105] Hay, David C. *Achieving Buzzword Compliance* (Basking Ridge, NJ: Technics Publications, 2018.

overview model contains the unified business ontology, roughly analogous to what I'm calling the domain model (or the business subject area model). The semantic models, which contain business unit-specific divergences from the overview model, correspond to sub-domain models. Then (3) the essential model (derived from the overview model) acts as a sort of unified field theory, which ties together the individual semantic (sub-domain) models in a way that makes sense in the context of the high-level business constructs contained in the overview model. It is the essential model that is used to create the logical and physical data models and eventual implementation.[106]

It is impossible to effectively support Domain-Driven Design without having an overarching, business-focused domain model lending support and context to the individual sub-domain models that support process-centered data structures and messaging. We also need higher-level canonical models for the data entities that span domains, and at least a high-level enterprise conceptual model.

TANSTAAFL

In summary, to be successful at domain-driven development requires that you have a solid strategy in at least five areas:

- Domain-oriented data modeling and database development.
- Canonical data modeling.
- Some sort of service-oriented architecture, such as an Enterprise Service Bus (ESB) or ESB hub, that supports messaging and services.
- Master data management (and data governance, generally).
- Data warehousing (for organization-wide reporting and analytics).

---

[106] As I understand it, the Overview Model is a conceptual model intended for high-level business audiences; the Essential Model is a more fully-articulated data model that can be "rolled over" into implementable Logical and Physical models. The Essential Model ties together the various Semantic models, and ensures they conform to the business understanding of the data captured in the Overview Model. In my mind, the Semantic models correspond to Domain and Subdomain models, and the Essential models are canonical models.

As we have seen, even with Domain-Driven Development and the use of microservices, you will not be able to avoid the issue of canonical data, at least not indefinitely. At some point, you will have to address the issue of multiple, overlapping canonical data structures and "N * N Connections", the issue of Master Data, and the issue of how to support organization-wide analytics and reporting.[107]

What this comes down to, in the end, is a simple fact. At the root of all of our architecture and design choices is a simple fundamental principle of economics: TANSTAAFL (There Ain't No Such Thing As A Free Lunch). We may decide to forego planning and provisioning of canonical data to save us some up-front work in data design and application development. Still, we will end up paying for that choice later when we have to refactor canonical data structures to support MDM, data governance activities, or organizational reporting and analytics.

Pay now, or pay later.

(XML, English)

```xml
<location>
 <street>A-Street</street>
 <number>123a</number>
 <city>Atown</city>
 <country>United States</country>
 <continent>North America</continent>
</location>
<location>
 <street>B-Straat</street>
 <number>456b</number>
 <city>Bdam</city>
 <country>The Netherlands</country>
 <continent>Europe</continent>
</location>
```

---

[107] There's another issue we haven't talked about: support for the databases. The DDD approach assumes that each application team supports its own database(s). If, however, your organization has a DBA (Database Administration) group, they will almost certainly resist the additional support burden this approach will create.

(XML, English)

```
<Address zip_code="93657">A-Street 123a, 93657, Atown</Address>
<Address zip_code="1234 AB" country_code="nl">B-Straat 456b,
 Bdam</Address>
```

(CSV, English)

```
Country;State;City;Street;Number;
USA;California;Atown;A-Street;123a;
NLD;;Bdam;B-Straat;456b;
```

(JSON, Dutch)

```
{"adres":
 {"landcode":1, "postcode":"93657", "woonplaats": "Atown",
 "straat": "A-Street", "nr":"123a"}
},
{"adres":
 {"landcode":31, "postcode":"1234 AB", "woonplaats": "Bdam",
 "straat": "B-Straat", "nr":"456b"}
}
```

Figure 7a: Multiply-Defined Address Data

```
<element name="Addresses" type="tns:tAddresses"/>
<complexType name="Addresses">
 <sequence>
 <element name="Address" type="tns:tAddress" minOccurs="0"
   maxOccurs="unbounded"/>
 </sequence>
</complexType>
<complexType name="tAddress">
 <sequence>
 <element name="Street" type="string" minOccurs="0"
   maxOccurs="1"/>
 <element name="Number" type="string" minOccurs="0"
   maxOccurs="1"/>
 <element name="ZipCode" type="string" minOccurs="0"
   maxOccurs="1"/>
 <element name="City" type="string" minOccurs="0" maxOccurs="1"/>
 <element name="State" type="string" minOccurs="0" maxOccurs="1"/>
 <element name="CountryCode" type="tns:tCountryCode" minOccurs="0"
   maxOccurs="1"/>
 <element name="ContinentCode" type="tns:tContinentCode"
   minOccurs="0" maxOccurs="1"/>
 </sequence>
```

```
</complexType>
<simpleType name="tCountryCode">
<!-- no fixed enum, because countries is not a fixed set in time.
    -->
 <restriction base="string">
 <pattern value="[A-Z]{2}"/>
 </restriction>
</simpleType>
<simpleType name="tContinentCode">
 <restriction base="string">
 <enumeration value="AF"/><!-- Africa -->
 <enumeration value="AN"/><!-- Antarctica -->
 <enumeration value="AS"/><!-- Asia -->
 <enumeration value="EU"/><!-- Europe -->
 <enumeration value="NA"/><!-- North America -->
 <enumeration value="OC"/><!-- Oceania -->
 <enumeration value="SA"/><!-- South America -->
 </restriction>
</simpleType>
```

Figure 7b: Canonical Address Model (XSD, English)

```
<Addresses>
 <Address>
 <Street>A-Street</Street>
 <Number>123a</Number>
 <ZipCode>93657</ZipCode>
 <City>Atown</City>
 <State>California</State>
 <CountryCode>US</CountryCode>
 <ContinentCode>NA</ContinentCode>
 </Address>
 <Address>
 <Street>B-Straat</Street>
 <Number>456b</Number>
 <ZipCode>1234 AB</ZipCode>
 <City>Bdam</City>
 <CountryCode>NL</CountryCode>
 <ContinentCode>EU</ContinentCode>
 </Address>
</Addresses>
```

Figure 7c: Canonical Address Data (XML, English)

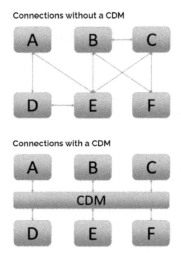

Connections without a CDM

Connections with a CDM

In this example, you need 16 translations when you do not use a CDM. With a CDM, you need only 12.

Figure 7d: Number of Connections With and Without a CDM

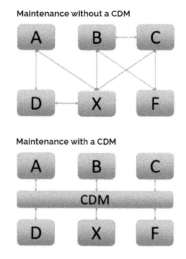

Maintenance without a CDM

Maintenance with a CDM

Figure 7e: Translation Maintenance With and Without a CDM

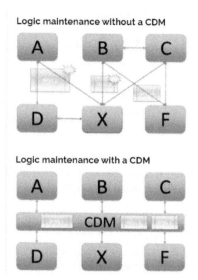

Logic maintenance without a CDM

Logic maintenance with a CDM

Figure 7f: Logic Maintenance With and Without a CDM

Key Points

- Domain-Driven Development (DDD) separates data into multiple persistence stores, each supporting a particular business sub-domain and a set of associated services and messages.

- The DDD approach is intended to increase the velocity of application development and eliminate the problem of defining data the same way across multiple business domains, each of which may have its own definitions for particular data entities like *Customer* or *Product*.

- Data modeling for DDD involves creating a domain-level data model with separate subject areas or diagrams for the associated sub-domains. This ensures that entities and attributes used across different sub-domains are defined consistently (and reused as much as possible).

- It's important for the data modeler to ask questions to determine where similar entities in different sub-domains are the same things or different things.

- It's also important to identify which of several similar entities and/or attributes contain the canonical data to use for organization-wide analytics and reporting.

- A canonical data model is very helpful in creating a translation layer that allows services to communicate between applications that define and persist data in different ways. A canonical model also defines organizational data that spans multiple domains.

- Define and model your data at as high a level as possible, then reuse data entities in lower-level domain and subdomain models. Implement only what you need in a given database to support an application or set of services.

- Eventually, the DDD approach will require the creation of some sort of canonical database and/or MDM repository. It will probably also require the creation of a data warehouse or data mart for reporting and analytics. It is best to plan and prepare for these eventualities ahead of time rather than wait until needed.

Chapter 16
In Search of Meaning

They have been at a great feast of languages and stolen the scraps.

William Shakespeare

In the next section of this book, we are going to explore the question of whether – and how – data modeling might be considered to be a design activity rather than a simple description of existing data assets. First, though, I would like to take a fairly high-level look at the question of *semantics* and *ontologies*,[108] which are central to the practice of data modeling.

As already noted, many, if not most, data modeling practitioners advocate starting with an enterprise-level understanding of business terms and processes. At the same time, data modelers also make use of enterprise-level data model patterns as a starting point for their modeling activities. This is what one might call a "top-down" approach to modeling data. The domain-centered approach

---

[108] *Semantics* is the study of the meaning of words, and the attempt to develop a shared understanding of meaning using words. An *ontology* is a formal representation of this shared understanding, defined by formal rules. It may be asserted, for example, that the description of entities, attributes, and relationships in a data model is an ontology that captures the semantics (i.e., the shared understanding) of some area of the business.

used in Domain-Driven Development (as seen in the previous chapter) would be called a "bottom-up" approach[109] to modeling.

DIFFERING SEMANTIC VIEWPOINTS

We've already noted two areas where differing semantic viewpoints can occur. First, the realization that as we attempt to "model the business", what we are really modeling are the various understandings of business users about how the business works, which may not be correct. Second, two (or more) different business areas may have conflicting understandings. For example, the conflicting views of how warranties work held by the Contract and Claims groups. As I mentioned earlier, the problem with the "bottom-up" approach to modeling is that it doesn't surface these conflicting viewpoints and gives us a chance to reconcile them. This, in turn, can cause important business data requirements to remain unsurfaced, undiscussed, and unmodeled. Advocates of Domain-Driven Design may assert that these higher-level understandings can eventually be "harvested" from the lower-level sub-domain models, but this would only happen if someone had occasion to ask the right questions!

In my mind, the advantage of a "top-down" approach to modeling is that it allows the maximum number of pertinent questions to be asked of the largest number of affected business stakeholders. Modeling from at least the domain (i.e., business subject area) level downward will allow the data modeler to see where there is general agreement on business meanings and processes, and to identify and discuss disagreements to see whether they are legitimate differences or simply misunderstandings or differences in vernacular. Where legitimate differences in business meaning exist, a portion of the domain model can be split off into appropriate sub-domains. The "bottom-up" approach enables us to create databases (persistence stores) more quickly, but the "top-down" approach gives us the opportunity to create the largest possible shared understanding of

---

[109] Or, perhaps, "middle-out" would be a more appropriate description.

the business among the affected business stakeholders, and thus the largest possible degree of data reuse.[110]

MODELING "TRUE" VS. "GOOD" STORIES

Graeme Simsion[111] has noted that disagreements exist within the data modeling community as to whether data models merely describe reality, or whether they can, in fact, create (at least in part) a reality that hasn't previously existed.[112] Similarly, there are differences between people who believe that data models describe an absolute objective reality and those who believe that data models capture only subjective understandings of reality.[113] And among objectivists (people who believe that data models reflect an absolute reality), there is disagreement about whether this reality can be modeled in only one correct way, or in many possible ways.[114]

These differences stem, in large part, from differences in viewpoint about what a data model is and what it should be used for. As I mentioned at the beginning of this book, how you define a data model determines the value that a data model will contribute, both to a given project and to the organization as a whole (remember what I said about Great Northern Airlines!). When attempting to justify the value of data modeling to application developers, I often hear that data models are not needed if the end goal is merely to produce a schema for a

---

[110] See my explanation of the concept of "Modeling Up and Building Down" in the previous chapter.

[111] See Simsion's Data Modeling Theory and Practice, p. 5.

[112] People who believe data models only reflect reality are called interpretivists; people who believe that data models can create reality are called positivists.

[113] These are called objectivists and subjectivists, respectively.

[114] These are called semantic absolutists and semantic relativists, respectively.

database or other data persistence store. And this is probably true.[115] However, if the goal is to produce a shared understanding of data requirements for a business domain, then a data model is essential! To quote Graeme Simsion again:

> *Atkins (1997) classifies data modeling definitions according to the objectivist/ subjectivist dichotomy, whether the focus is on modeling reality or data, and whether the purpose is infological (stakeholder communications) or datalogical (database specification), and also notes that data modeling may be characterized as either analysis [i.e., descriptive only] or design.*[116]

To me, the solution is clear: We should define "data modeling" in terms of what will contribute the most value, both now and in the future. We don't want to define "data modeling" as "the operating of trains"!

This is why I've distinguished, in this book, between "true stories" and "good stories". A "true story" is an accurate representation of the world that we have chosen to live in and do business in. It may not be an Absolutist depiction of objective reality, but, like James Gatz's "Jay Gatsby", it is a conception that we "remain faithful to until the end".[117] In this sense, the data modeler functions as a sort of behavioral therapist.[118] In therapy, the job is not to impose on the patient an Absolutist view of reality, but rather to make the client aware of assumptions and misconceptions he/she may have and to enable him/her to make clear and

---

[115] Graeme Simsion, however, has argued that even if there is not a visible "artifact" for the data model, the developer who "just" creates a database still has a data model in his or her head!

[116] Ibid.

[117] See F. Scott Fitzgerald's *The Great Gatsby*.

[118] I draw a number of lessons in data modeling practice from the discipline of Cognitive Behavioral Therapy, or CBT. For a brief but instructive overview of this discipline, see Judy Beck's "10 Principles of Cognitive Behavioral Therapy (CBT)" at https://bit.ly/3znsZnf.

informed choices about the world. The ultimate goal is to enable the client to function effectively in the world, not to understand everything about it.

Similarly, a "good story" is one in which we can move quickly and effectively from the present that we now inhabit, to a future in which our dreams and visions are achieved. It's the "happily ever after" part of the story. Again, in this sense, the data modeler functions as a behavioral therapist, enabling business stakeholders to chart their own vision of the future and to see what sorts of assumptions and choices might be constraining their ability to respond quickly and effectively to changing business climates, marketplaces, and technologies. As I said before, a good data model not only describes the current state, or philosophy, of the business; it provides a pathway forward into a better future state.

In my view, the job of the data modeler is not so much the describing of reality to the business as it is the enabling of the business to function effectively within the reality it has chosen; to tell the story that it wants to tell to the world, both now and in the future.

MODELING "THE BUSINESS"

How does this shift in perspective (from the data model as a description of the business to the data model as enabler of the business) help answer our questions about how (or whether) data models capture meaning about reality?

First of all, as I've already asserted, data models don't capture objective reality per se. Instead, they capture the assumptions and choices we've made about the reality we've chosen to accept. Take, for example, two different manufacturing companies: One company manufactures a limited number of product models, each having a set of standard options and with very little customization allowed. The other allows prospective customers to custom-order a product with almost limitless customization options. The first company will deliver new models more quickly and cheaply, with lower manufacturing costs. The second company will have higher development and manufacturing costs but will capture a market segment where people are willing to pay higher prices for more customized products. These are two different and distinct choices, and neither of them is "right" or "wrong". The data models for these two companies will tell the story of the choices they have made and the segment of the market they have chosen to sell to. The data models will also capture assumptions these companies have made about how new products are brought to market, how products are sold to customers, how post-sales customer support should be handled, and so on. The job of the data modeler is not to impose a particular view of Reality on the business stakeholders, nor to accept their view of Reality as Gospel truth. Rather, the job of the data modeler is to help business stakeholders see and understand the choices they have made, the assumptions behind those choices, and the possible consequences of those choices on the company's ability to satisfy its customers (and other stakeholders) and achieve its present and future objectives. In short, the job of the data modeler is not to "model the (reality of) the business", but to enable the business to understand the consequences of the reality it has chosen to accept.

Graeme Simsion refers to the arena of reality covered by a data model as the *Universe of Discourse* (UoD).[119] That is, a data model encompasses not a subset of reality per se but rather a subset of the reality we've chosen to talk about. It is, to use an earlier analogy, the landscape of the story, the "setup" for the tale that is being told. It introduces the cast of characters, describes their motivations, and sets up the plot, so that all readers of the story (or hearers of the tale) have a common basis for understanding the twists and turns of the plot as it unfolds. To quote Simsion again, a data model is "a reasonably inclusive framework for locating arguments and assumptions, rather than a methodology."[120]

---

[119] Ibid, p. 34. I will also refer to this concept throughout this Chapter as the "Domain of Discourse" (DoD).

[120] Ibid, pp. 34-35. Also, it's worth looking at Figure 3-1 in Simsion's book ("Stages in Database Design – A Generic Framework"), which shows how a subset of the Universe of Discourse (which he calls a *Perceived UoD*)

An interesting example of this came about when I was asked to create a data model for government-mandated Greenhouse Gas (GHG) regulatory reporting. Unfortunately, even though the government had mandated the reporting, set a strict deadline for it, and even imposed penalties for missing the deadline, it had failed to create instructions for what was to be reported, or how reporting was to be done. Our business stakeholders (which included the head of the department responsible for regulatory compliance, plus heads of our various divisional engineering departments) and I had to create a data model of how we thought the government would eventually require regulatory reporting to be done, and made it flexible enough to accommodate any changes the government would eventually make. Some of the entities in the model were "reality-based"; for example, we modeled the regulatory classifications the government had already published. Other entities were modeled out of whole cloth; for example, the entities needed to support anticipated tasks such as "scoring" emissions and managing GHG "credits". What we created was not so much a model of regulatory reporting requirements as it was a model of how we intended to address those requirements whenever they were issued. It modeled the "domain of discourse", rather than the domain itself.

Another example is when I was asked to create a data model for the management of product sales options. I asked what the process of managing sales options was and what the business rules were. I was told that the process hadn't been developed yet (this was a new business process, with a new supporting application). At the same time, they said they needed the data model right away! So I asked them for as much information as they had on sales options and how they worked, and I created a provisional data model. This data model became the jumping-off point for a series of discussions with the business about how the process was supposed to work, and the data model was continually modified as

---

becomes captured in Conceptual and Logical data models, then a Physical Design, and finally an External Schema Specification.

the discussions continued. In this case, the purpose of the data model was not so much to "model the business" as it was to enable the business to model itself!

We see examples of "conceptual" (as opposed to reality-based) data modeling in the "abstract entities" that are part of almost every universal data model pattern. Take, for example, the ubiquitous *Party* entity. Unless you work in a law office, you will almost never hear a business user refer to a company stakeholder as a "Party". Yet, we data modelers almost universally use "Party" as a logical supertype of a company stakeholder (Customer, Supplier, Dealer, etc.). This is a made-up concept, yet it helps us (and our fellow travelers in the domain of discourse) visualize and discuss the relationships that may exist between our organization's various stakeholders. So, because it helps drive the conversation and facilitate understanding, we include it in the model.[121]

This brings me to the reiteration of another point I made earlier: the value of a data model is not in the way that it purports to represent reality. The value of a data model lies in how it enables a group of stakeholders to understand a problem (or business opportunity), discuss it, reach agreement on a course of action, and execute the plan to achieve the goal. It is analogous to the value of a map: the map itself is an inaccurate depiction of geographical reality; its value lies in its ability to empower us to get from one destination to another.

So let's keep this in mind as we build our data models. What the business needs from us is not a semantically correct depiction of reality; they need a way to understand how to get from where they are now to where they want to be.

---

[121] I personally prefer the term "Business Partner", and use this concept in my canonical models.

Key Points

- Modeling from the "top-down" (i.e., starting from an enterprise or business subject area view of the business), allows the data modeler to see where there is general agreement on business meanings and processes and to identify and discuss disagreements to see whether they are legitimate differences or simply misunderstandings or differences in vernacular.

- Where differences in business meaning exist, part of the domain model can be split off to an appropriate sub-domain model. This gives the data modeler an opportunity to create the largest possible shared understanding of the business among the affected business stakeholders and thus the largest possible degree of data reuse.

- The value of a data model is not in the way that it purports to represent reality. The value of a data model lies in the way it enables a group of stakeholders to understand a problem (or business opportunity), discuss it, reach an agreement on a course of action, and execute the plan to achieve the goal.

- The area of reality covered by a data model (known as the *Universe of Discourse* or *Domain of Discourse*) is not a subset of reality per se, but rather a subset of the reality we've chosen to talk about. A data model is "a reasonably inclusive framework for locating arguments and assumptions, rather than a methodology."

- The data modeler functions as a sort of behavioral therapist: in therapy, the job is not to impose on the patient an absolutist view of reality, but rather to make the client aware of assumptions and misconceptions he/she may have and to enable him/her to make clear and informed choices about the world.

- The job of the data modeler is to help business stakeholders see and understand the choices they have made, the assumptions behind those choices, and the possible consequences of those choices on the company's ability to satisfy its customers (and other stakeholders) and achieve its present and future objectives.

- We should define "data modeling" in terms of what will contribute the most value to the business, both now and in the future. What the business needs from us is not a semantically correct depiction of reality; they need a way to understand how to get from where they are now to where they want to be.

Yeah let's do something crazy,
Something absolutely wrong
While we're waiting for the miracle, for the miracle to come.

Leonard Cohen, Waiting for the Miracle[122]

W hen my good friend John Giles reviewed the first draft of this book, he noted the number of places that the word "project" is used. The problem with a project-focused approach to data modeling is, of course, that the "big picture" (that is, the needs of the enterprise) may be lost if data modeling isn't done at the enterprise level.

In smaller companies, especially those with an awareness of their enterprise-level data needs and problems, organization-wide data and BI initiatives should certainly be pursued and encouraged. Nothing I've said in my books about doing data work on projects or modeling at the domain (or Business Subject Area) level should be construed as advocating against an enterprise-level view of data.

---

[122] Graeme Simsion uses this quote to preface Chapter 3 of *Data Modeling Theory and Practice*.

But what if you work for a massive organization, especially if its operations are diverse. Is there even such a thing as an "enterprise" view? I work for a global, Fortune 200 manufacturing organization that is a collection of smaller, independent companies. Getting corporate-level support for enterprise-wide data and BI initiatives is very difficult.[123] After almost 30 years, we are finally just starting to dip our big toes into the waters of data governance, data quality, and master data management.

Almost all the work I've done in the past quarter-century has been project-focused. My challenge has been doing project-focused data modeling and database work in a way that enables, rather than obstructs, larger organizational data and BI initiatives if and when they occur.

So, on the one hand, a small organization may easily embrace a single, unified "enterprise" view, while some larger organizations may not even try! John tells a story that demonstrates the benefits in challenging what constitutes an "enterprise":

One of my clients was a huge state government department. Buried deep within it was a Fire Management group, responsible for minimizing the risks from wildfires. Their scope had almost nothing to do with the overall department, and there was no attempt to model the department as a whole. Conversely, when wildfires broke out, a virtual organization formed. It potentially could involve people from up to 17 other organizations, including members from a volunteer fire authority, the state police force, ambulance groups, and many more.

A shared model was desired to facilitate data sharing across the diverse organizations. The need for this was highlighted after a particularly tragic day where many lives were lost. An enquiry followed, not to appoint blame, but to learn. Apparently one incident

---

[123] It's interesting to note that even though Graeme Simsion notes the value of Enterprise-level modeling in his book, he omits it from the Practice section because "actual use of and fidelity to enterprise models in practice is the exception rather than the rule" (p. 37).

controller asked a representative of the volunteer fire authority how many fire trucks were available. The reply was, "We don't have 'fire trucks'. We have 'appliances'. Is that what you mean?"

The frustrated incident controller turn to the government department's logistics officer and asked, "Well, how many fire trucks (or if you prefer, 'appliances') do you have?" The response was, "We don't have either. We have tankers and slip-ons. Which do you mean?" (By the way, 'appliances' and 'tankers' are effectively the same thing, and 'slip-ons' are four-wheel-drive vehicles with a tank-and-pump unit "slipped on").

The very frustrated incident controller is reported as shouting, "I don't care what you call them. How many vehicles that can squirt water have you got?"

What are some of the lessons that we can learn here?

First, a common language is important; in some cases, a life and death matter. One of the greatest values of a data model is giving people a common vocabulary to use when discussing business needs, problems and opportunities.

Second, the "enterprise" behind an enterprise model can be, like in my organization, a discrete member of the larger group, or, as in John's case, it can actually be larger than any single organization.

Third, even if your organization is huge and complex (like John's virtual organization), if sharing of data is important, you may simply need to work towards a single enterprise view.

But no matter the size of the organization, seek to reflect what the "business" defines as the appropriate size.

ADDRESSING THE DILEMMA

Our IT data services organization recognized this dilemma early on and addressed it in the following ways:

- All data modeling is done at the business subject area (i.e., domain) level to make both data models and databases as business-focused and reusable as possible.

- All entities and attributes are defined in business rather than application terms, and data-related business rules are captured in the data model and implemented in the database.

- When modeling for a new project, we check to see whether requested data Entities have already been modeled and implemented for other projects, and we try to reuse these models and data structures as much as possible.

- Databases are not regarded as merely persistence containers for application-specific data but as repositories of business data that can be used for any legitimate business purpose.

- Databases don't just store data; they also enforce business data definitions and rules, and support data-related processing.

- We enforce a number of database design rules to ensure high data quality, naming consistency, good performance, and ease of maintenance. Among these are the use of Fundamental Stored Procedures (FSPs) – also known as "CRUD" procedures – to help ensure transactional integrity, support optimistic concurrency, and prevent unauthorized data updates. All database updating must be done through the FSPs; direct updating of tables by applications or database users is not permitted.

- DDL to generate database schemas, constraints, and other database objects is generated directly from our modeling tool, using macro code. The FSPs are auto-generated from the database schema, using a special program we've written.

- We set up classes to educate our business and IT stakeholders about our data modeling and database design standards, and the reasons behind them. The classes for business people are called *Clear Thinking About Data* (CTAD); the classes for IT people are called *Database Information Exchange* (DBIX).

Since, as I noted earlier, our company has always done organizational reporting and analytics directly from our transactional databases (i.e., we don't have an enterprise data warehouse), this approach gives our business users the best chance of getting useful, accurate, and business-relevant data for their business purposes.

"Working Toward"

This incremental approach to data modeling and database implementation was described, in *Growing Business Intelligence*, using a phrase from landscape designer Ann Lovejoy: "Working Toward". The idea is that it's seldom possible to do everything you want to do all at once, so you have to map out a strategy that allows you to achieve your immediate goals while incrementally working toward your ultimate, long-range objective.

When *Growing Business Intelligence* came out, I got an earful from Data and BI professionals who were incensed that I wasn't advocating an immediate, full-blown, EDW implementation. The fact is, our company has never had an EDW, and never will. The idea of enterprise data warehousing is a complete non-starter at our company, so we've had to adopt other strategies (such as a data lake, with some data governance, data quality, and MDM tools). With each iteration, the idea is to get a "quick win" for the company, thus showing the soundness of our approach, and then use this success to get management approval and funding for the next iteration. At a lot of companies, you're not going to get funding for a "home run"; you have to show you can get on base first!

As I explained in a previous chapter, my approach is to "Model Upward"; that is, determine which entities can be appropriately modeled at a domain (business subject area) level or higher. For example, the following figure (Figure 8) shows the hierarchy of models I use in my latest project. While creating the subdomain models for database implementation, I can draw from (and update as needed) any of the higher-level data models.

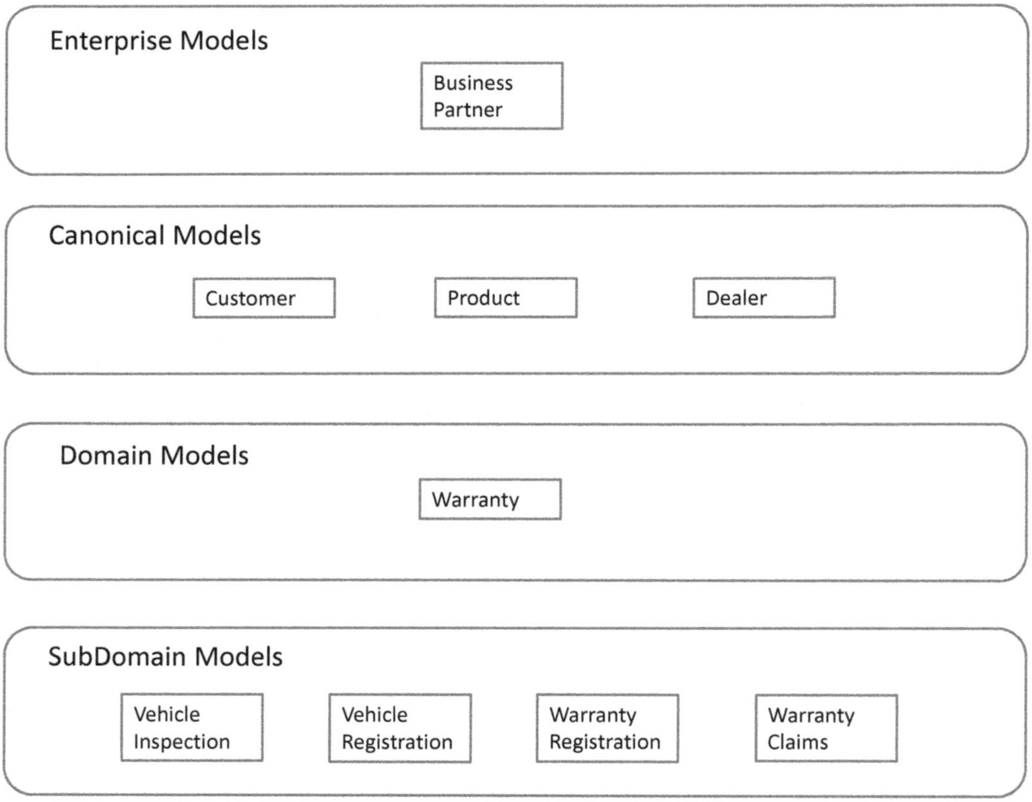

Figure 8: Hierarchy of Models for a Warranty Project.

ONWARD AND UPWARD

So how do we get from a domain view of data to an enterprise view of data? There are a number of possible approaches; your organization may use one or more:

- If your organization supports an EDW, then you can use your domain-level (and higher) data models to implement an EDW one domain at a time; the resulting EDW data model will (over time) become your enterprise data model.

- Alternatively, your domain-level models might be used to create a set of domain-specific data marts for reporting and analytics, using transactional data migrated from on-prem databases into a data lake in the cloud.

- If your organization supports an Enterprise Service Bus (ESB), and uses messaging for Enterprise Application Integration (EAI), then your domain-level (and canonical) models can be used to create canonical messaging schemas to support the consistent transfer of data between applications and services. These canonical schemas can translate data between disparate application data schemas. Also, in cases where multiple services need to reference the same master data, you can begin the creation of a canonical (i.e., master) database on the ESB Hub to store this data.

- If your organization is creating a data lake populated with data migrated from application databases, your domain-level data models can be used to help create a business-meaningful, integrated view-layer over the raw data, making it more cohesive and easier to consume by end-user reporting and analysis tools.

- If your organization supports a Master Data (MDM) repository, you can use your domain-level models to iteratively create and implement your MDM repository with customer, product, dealer and other canonical data. Then the MDM repository can be used to "push" this data to application databases, the ESB Hub, etc. An MDM initiative is also a good way to get your organization started down the road of data governance.

- Domain-level data models can also support enterprise-wide data governance and data quality initiatives. They show, for example, what areas of the business use or update which types of data, and they show what data quality rules have been defined. Metadata from data models will show exactly where certain types of data, such as customer or product data, are used across multiple applications and business units.

Data modelers and other data professionals in a given organization need to be constantly on the lookout for opportunities to promote the application of data models and data rules to higher levels of the organization in support of initiatives such as business intelligence, MDM, data quality, data governance, and the like.

I encourage data professionals to be constantly on the lookout for opportunities to model and implement, if possible, higher-level views of organizational data. If a new town is to be built with integrated services, nobody would dump 1,000 tradespeople into an open area armed with materials and tools without a town plan. The town plan doesn't need to specify the color of the tiles in the bathroom for the town hall; that detail can be left for later. But at least a high level sketch would help.

In a similar manner, while initiatives within the organization may be driven by separate projects, or different business groups, investing in a light-weight 'town plan' (such as an enterprise-level conceptual model or canonical data model) provides a sensible and cost-effective foundation for future modeling work.

As I've said, data models contribute great value at the project level, but it's important to understand that they also have value to contribute to higher-level Data and BI initiatives, as well!

Key Points

- Depending on the structure and priorities of a given organization, it may not be possible, or even wise, to do enterprise-level data modeling or similar organization-wide data or BI initiatives. Let the business define the size and shape of the "enterprise".

- Where a single enterprise view does not exist, it is necessary to adopt a "working toward" approach, doing project-level or domain-level modeling and implementation in ways that will support (rather than obstruct) enterprise-wide data and BI initiatives if and when, they occur. Nonetheless, strive to articulate a single unifying "town plan" for whatever the business decides is the scope of your "organization".

- Both this book and *Growing Business Intelligence* give examples of using a pattern-based approach to iteratively move an organization from its current state to a more enterprise-focused view of data and BI. Chart a course toward your desired future state, and craft a series of interim "pattern" states to achieve it.

- Model and implement data so that it has business meaning and relevance at whatever level it is implemented and can easily be reused at other levels of the organization.

- Domain-level data models can support many enterprise-wide data and BI initiatives, such as data warehouses, data marts, data lakes, ESB hubs, canonical messaging schemas, MDM repositories, data quality programs, and organizational data governance.

Section IV
Data Modeling and Design Thinking

Great things are not done by impulse, but by a series of small things brought together.

Vincent van Gogh

One of the oft-asked (and seldom really answered) questions in the profession of data modeling is this: can data modeling be considered a design activity? Graeme Simsion explores some of these design questions in his seminal book on data modeling,[124] specifically the question of whether data model is a *descriptive* activity or a *design* activity. In Simsion's mind, the answer seems to depend on whether data modeling is properly thought of as an exercise in (data) requirements analysis or as something more than that. Are our data models merely representations of concepts that already exist independently in the real world, or are they representations of concepts that did not exist before the model was created? Simsion quotes from W. Kent[125] the argument that what we are modeling is not reality itself but the way in which

---

[124] Simsion, Graeme. *Data Modeling Theory and Practice* (New Jersey: Technics Publications, 2007), Chapter 3.

[125] Kent, W. *Data and Reality: Basic Assumptions in Data Processing Reconsidered* (Amsterdam, NY: North-Holland Pub. Co., 1978), p. 22.

information about reality is perceived and processed by people. Therefore, conceptual modeling can be looked upon as "a process of social construction",[126] in which new concepts can and will be created as part of the modeling process.

In my own mind, the answer to the "description vs. design" question depends upon where and when data modeling is done.[127] If requirements are developed first, and the data modeler is brought in merely to represent the data requirements in a form that lends itself to the creation of a database or some other data persistence store, then this is obviously a descriptive activity. If, however, the data modeler *actively participates* in the activity of requirements elicitation and elaboration, then the act of data modeling can be a design activity.

This concept is a key component of something that is called *Design Thinking*. In design thinking, designers aren't brought in mid-process to flesh out requirements that have already been created; they are brought in at the very beginning of the process to help define the scope and characteristics of the product! The former role is tactical; the latter role is strategic.

In the following chapters, we will explore the application of Human-Centered Design (HCD) and design thinking to data modeling, and see how these concepts can help transform data modeling from a descriptive activity to a design activity.

---

[126] Simsion, p. 41.

[127] Meaning, when is data modeling done within the application-development, system-development or process-development process.

Thinking about Design is hard, but not thinking about it can be disastrous.

Ralph Caplan

The concept of design thinking originated with David Kelley, the founder of a Silicon Valley company called IDEO.[128] The idea behind design thinking is to move designers from a tactical role (making an already-developed idea more attractive to consumers) to a more strategic role (helping to define the idea itself). Or, to put it another way, moving the arena of design work from "What is the best way to do this thing?" to "What is the best thing to do?"

I've alluded to this already in previous sections of this book: the idea that a data model can drive conversations about what could or should be, rather than simply what is; the idea that a data model should tell a *good story* (about how things should be) and not just a *true story* (about what currently is); the idea that a data model can be a driver for process improvement. These are all *design* concepts!

---

[128] For more information on IDEO and its work, reference their website at www.ideo.org.

Human-Centered Design (HCD) takes design thinking a step further: it makes the human experience the central focus of the design effort. As an early example, Tim Brown[129] uses the British engineer Isambard Kingdom Brunel, the designer of the Great Western Railway. Brunel designed the railway with an eye toward providing not only efficient transportation but the best possible "user experience". He kept his tracks on the flattest possible gradient, using bridges, viaducts, cuttings, and tunnels as necessary, so that passengers would have the sense of "floating across the countryside". He designed the railway around the experience that passengers would have riding the trains. We'll look at both of these concepts in more depth in a moment, but first, let's take a high-level look at what design is, generally.

CHARACTERISTICS OF DESIGN

Graeme Simsion[130] references the following "Properties of Design" (from Bryan Lawson[131]:

- Design problems cannot be comprehensively stated; some requirements will only become apparent as solutions are attempted and evaluated.

- Design problems require subjective interpretation; not everyone will see the problem, or the requirements, in the same way.

- Design problems tend to be organized hierarchically. In other words, a given design problem can be organized into sub-problems, each of which is, itself, a design problem.

---

[129] Brown, Tim. *Change by Design* (New York, NY: Harper-Collins, 2009).

[130] *Data Modeling Theory and Practice*, pp. 29, 63-87.

[131] Lawson, Bryon. *How Designers Think: The Design Process Demystified* (Second Edition) (Oxford, Architectural Press, 1983).

- There is no single solution to a design problem. Different people working from the same set of requirements will find different solutions to a given design problem.

- Design problems need to be solved *holistically*. That is, with an awareness of the context in which the problem exists.[132] For example, when using data model patterns, data modelers need to be aware that the same pattern cannot blindly be applied to all similar problems; rather, the pattern may need to be modified somewhat in response to the particular circumstances of the problem or the goal that needs to be achieved.

- There is no one infallibly correct process that will always find the correct solution for a given set of design problems. Different approaches may need to be found based on the problem domain and other conditions.

- Design solutions involve finding, as well as solving, problems. As a problem is being solved, other problems will surface unexpectedly, and these problems must also be solved. Anyone who has ever done a home remodeling project knows how this works. It is this aspect of problem-solving that requires *creativity* on the part of the problem-solver.

- Design solutions involve having to make subjective *value judgements*. When faced with unexpected problems and multiple possible solutions, problem-solvers must exercise judgment in choosing an approach. The type(s) of approach(es) chosen by a given problem-solver over time become that person's *style* or trademark.

---

[132] This is often referred to as "Systems Thinking".

- Design solutions are *prescriptive* rather than descriptive. That is, they don't describe what is; instead, they seek to achieve what ought to be.

- Designers work in the context of a *need for action*. They create practical solutions to concrete problems in the context of time, budget, and resource constraints.

- Design solutions are a *contribution to knowledge*; that is, they can be reused (with caution) to solve future design problems. Data model patterns are an example of this.

Does data modeling fit this description of design activity? I would assert that it does. In my experience, especially doing data modeling work on Agile projects, I've found that a lot of data modeling is more exploratory than descriptive in nature. That is, the data model is the vehicle the business (or the project team) uses to wrap their heads around a business problem and develop a strategy for solving it. As we have noted, the data model becomes an artifact of what is called *conjecture-analysis*, in which requirements emerge through client feedback on proposed designs, and the data modeler becomes less of a business stenographer and more of a behavioral therapist, guiding business and project stakeholders to an awareness of their assumptions and choices and empowering them to chart their own course forward.

THE PROCESS OF DESIGN

Jeanne Liedtka and Tim Ogilvie have written a book called *Designing for Growth*[133] in which they lay out a process for design thinking based on four questions:

---

[133] Liedtka, Jeanne and Tim Ogilvie. *Designing for Growth* (New York, NY: Columbia Business School Publishing, 2011).

1) *What Is?* Understand the current problem or need in its broadest possible context, making sure that all stakeholders have an opportunity to articulate their needs and concerns.

2) *What If?* After gathering the necessary data and conducting stakeholder interviews, use a brainstorming process to generate a number of "outside the box" ideas. Put these ideas in the form of hypotheses, and evaluate them against your design criteria.

3) *What Wows?* While evaluating your ideas, look for the ones that hit the "sweet spot" where the maximum amount of stakeholder value can be delivered within the limits of the available resources and in a sustainable way.

4) *What Works?* Using prototypes, test out your best ideas in the real world with actual users. Iteratively rework the prototype based on user feedback. Fail early to succeed sooner.

We will see significant process parallels between the design thinking approach, Human-Centered Design (HCD), and Agile.

From a process perspective, design thinking aims to increase the number of choices available to designers (and managers as well) and encourage thinking outside of traditional strategies. As Tim Brown puts it, "We need new choices!"[134] Jeanne Liedtka uses New York's Central Park as an example of "outside the box" thinking.[135] Of all the proposals the City looked at, only the proposal of Frederick Law Olmstead and his team was accepted. The reason was the City's requirement that cross-town traffic be accommodated without destroying the pastoral feel of the park. This was regarded as an impossible requirement by most of the architects because they were thinking in 2-dimensional terms. Only

---

[134] *Change by Design*, p. 3.

[135] *Designing for Growth*, p. 8.

Olmstead realized they could think in 3 dimensions and put the city streets *underneath* the Park!

Jeanne Liedtka makes the point that design thinking is more than just a new methodology or a set of tools: "It involves helping individuals make a new set of choices: to seek deep insights and be user-driven, to keep looking for great solutions even after hitting upon a good one, to risk not getting it right the first time, to continue to try in the face of failure."[136]

In design thinking, we're encouraged to "see every problem as a possibility". Jeanne Liedtka uses the example of IKEA's founder, Ingvar Kamprad.[137] When irate customers stormed into his company's warehouse because there weren't enough employees to help them, Kamprad turned customer self-service into his company's business model. IKEA's customers pick up disassembled furniture from the company's warehouses, take them home and assemble them!

We need an approach to problem-solving that matches the challenges of our times. As Tim Brown puts it[138]:

It is hard to imagine a time when the challenges we faced so vastly exceeded the creative resources we have brought to bear on them. Aspiring innovators may have attended a "brainstorming" session or learned a few gimmicks and tricks, but rarely do these temporary placeholders make it to the outside world in the form of new products, services, or strategies.

---

[136] Liedtka, Jeanne, Andrew King and Kevin Bennett. *Solving Problems With Design Thinking* (New York, NY: Columbia Business School Publishing, 2013), p. 9.

[137] *Designing for Growth*, p. 8.

[138] *Change by Design*, p. 3.

We need an approach to innovation that is powerful, effective, and broadly accessible, that can be integrated into all aspects of business and society, and that individuals and teams can use to generate breakthrough ideas that are implemented and that therefore have an impact.

Obstacles to Design Thinking

Nevertheless, there are many obstacles to implementing design thinking in most organizations. Some of these obstacles are organizational, and some are people issues. Both Tim Brown and Jeanne Liedtka address these issues in their books[139]:

- Insofar as design thinking is an open-ended, open-minded, and iterative process, it will feel chaotic to those people experiencing it for the first time. They may feel that such a process will take longer to deliver results. However, when prototyping is being done and customers can see results more immediately, less time and money are spent on approaches that will ultimately prove to be unsuccessful. And, it enables customers to decide when the resulting product is "good enough".

- Conversely, just as design thinking may feel uncomfortable to managers, designers may feel constrained by the fact that design work occurs within the context of projects run by managers. They may feel that their creativity is being stifled by time and budget constraints. But, as we will see, designers need to be able to embrace the constraints inherent in design work, in particular the constraints of *feasibility* (what is functionally possible), *viability* (what the business can support), and *desirability* (what the customer needs and wants).

- In many organizations, "innovation" is confined to a small specific part of the company, and the innovation space is a highly desired and

---

[139] *Change by Design*, pp. 17-20. *Solving Problems with Design Thinking*, pp. 10-11.

hotly contested territory. Innovation is often discouraged in all parts of the organization that are not specifically associated with R&D (even within R&D, there are often conflicts between groups doing applied vs. "blue sky" research). It can be challenging to get an organization to accept "innovation thinking" in all of its departments.

- Also, there are ongoing arguments about *who* should be doing design work. Is this the province only of professional designers? Can other employees of the company (specifically, managers) be taught design techniques? What are the advantages (and possible disadvantages) of pushing out design thinking to a larger audience?

We will be exploring these questions later when we discuss how to apply design thinking principles to data work. For example, when considering the extent of the involvement of developers and other project stakeholders in data modeling work.

Key Points

- The goal of design thinking is to move designers from a tactical role (making an already-developed idea more attractive to consumers) to a more strategic role (helping to define the idea itself). Or, to put it another way, moving the arena of design work from "What is the best way to do this thing?" to "What is the best thing to do?"

- Human-Centered Design (HCD) takes design thinking a step further: it makes the human experience the central focus of the design effort.

- Design problems need to be solved *holistically,* with an awareness of the context in which the problem exists.

- There is no one infallibly correct process that will always find the correct solution for a given set of design problems. Different approaches may need to be found based on the problem domain and other conditions.

- Design solutions involve finding as well as solving problems. As a problem is being solved, other problems will surface unexpectedly, and these problems must also be solved.

- Design solutions are prescriptive rather than descriptive. That is, they don't describe what is; instead, they seek to achieve what ought to be.

- Designers work in the context of a need for action; they create practical solutions to concrete problems in the context of time, budget, and resource constraints.

- The design process created by Jeanne Liedtka and Tim Ogilvie is based on four questions: *What Is? What If? What Wows?* and *What Works?*

- There are often organizational and personal conflicts that hinder the acceptance of design thinking in companies.

Chapter 19
Human-Centered Design

People ignore design that ignores people.

Frank Chimero

As mentioned in the previous chapter, *Human-Centered Design* (HCD) takes design thinking a step further in making the human experience the central focus of the design effort. In Human-Centered Design, people come together to understand a problem and work out an acceptable solution. HCD is predicated on the belief that all human problems, no matter how intractable they may seem, are solvable and that the most effective solutions will come from the community of people most affected by the problem. As IDEO.org puts it: "Being a human-centered designer is about believing that as long as you stay grounded in what you've learned from people, your team can arrive at new solutions that the world needs".[140]

CHARACTERISTICS OF HUMAN-CENTERED DESIGN

Human-Centered Design (HCD) is an approach to practical problem-solving based on iterative implementations (i.e., prototyping) of design solutions

---

[140] *The Field Guide to Human-Centered Design* (IDEO.org, 2015), p. 3.

developed in collaboration with the people most directly affected by the problem.[141]

In HCD:

- We focus on empowering other people to create their own solutions to their own problems. Too often, we create solutions for ourselves and then force them on others with predictable results.[142] If people don't feel they have an ownership stake in the solution, the solution won't get used.

- We use collaboration to generate ideas (i.e., team brainstorming). We keep ideas focused, positive, and as visual as possible. We aim for quantity of ideas over quality (avoid passing judgment) and evaluate them later.

- We prototype solutions iteratively and refactor them based on end-user feedback. A prototype doesn't have to be "market ready"; it might be a rough model of paper, wood, cardboard or clay. It just needs to work well enough to elicit useful feedback. One team prototyped a mobile financial application by creating a "Loan Surprise" dice game and getting people to play it.[143]

- We learn from current failures to ensure future success. I just saw a comic strip that said, "The Secret to Success – Don't Fail!" However, in HCD, failure is the most important part of success, provided that we fail quickly (before investing too much time and money) and that

---

[141] You can see several examples of the practical application of HCD to real-world situations at the IDEO.org website: https://www.ideo.org/perspectives.

[142] The failure of many Western attempts to solve Third-World problems is the origin of many jokes about "Solar-powered Cuisinarts" and such.

[143] *The Field Guide to Human-Centered Design*, p. 48.

the failure is instructive. Failures show us what doesn't work and, hopefully, guide us to solutions that do. In Ethiopia, for example, a design team was prototyping a planting machine for grain seeds, but the machine's wheels kept bogging down in the muddy soil. A local machine shop came up with the idea of wrapping the wheels in burlap, which enabled the machine to traverse the muddy fields.[144]

- We take a holistic approach to problem-solving. For example, when a workshop on community health was conducted with villagers in rural Nigeria, a team quickly discovered that their concern with health was more closely tied to concerns about diet, exercise, family, and community than about medicine or access to doctors.[145]

- We quickly discard ideas that don't work to make room for creative alternatives. For example, a team in Kenya had the idea of creating a call center for farmers to answer questions about agricultural problems and get information on new agricultural techniques. They "prototyped" this solution by collecting questions from the farmers and bringing in an agriculturist for one day to return the calls and answer the questions. They determined that the "call center" approach was not an ideal solution and ended up creating a series of short, instructional videos for the farmers.[146]

Tim Brown[147] draws an analogy between HCD and gardening (gardening analogies are among my favorites, as readers of *Growing Business Intelligence* know). He regards HCD as the art of "planting, tending, pruning and

---

[144] *The Field Guide to Human-Centered Design*, p. 112.

[145] *The Field Guide to Human-Centered Design*, p. 62.

[146] *The Field Guide to Human-Centered Design*, p. 120.

[147] Brown, Tim. *Change by Design* (HarperCollins, 2009), p. 74.

harvesting" ideas. And these ideas are created and nurtured in the service of some vision or goal. As gardening expert Ann Lovejoy says, "gardening by design" means "taking into account our patterns of living, how we want to be in the garden, and what we want the garden to do for us".[148] Good garden designs "have an elegant simplicity that makes them visually and emotionally pleasing even before a single plant is placed."[149] They take into consideration the particular features and characteristics of the site (soil type(s), drainage patterns, proportion of sun to shade, and so on). They blend naturally into their environment. They are of the right size and scale for their surroundings. They are easily accessible and inviting to navigate, with different "rooms" that satisfy different needs. They combine the right amount of inclusion (e.g. entertainment areas) with the right amount of privacy (e.g. meditation areas).

Finally, but most importantly, a good garden design is *sustainable*; that is, as the years go by, the benefits of the garden increase (as the landscape matures) but the amount of work and expense to maintain it decreases. A well-designed landscape requires less fertilizing, less watering, and less overall maintenance with each passing year.

The design principles that Ann Lovejoy espouses for gardening and landscaping are the same design principles at the core of Human-Centered Design.

HCD AND AGILE

As you can see, there are also close parallels between HCD and Agile. Both are collaborative and iterative processes in which creativity and experimentation are encouraged (within reasonable limits). Both acknowledge that all requirements cannot be determined ahead of time, and that provision must be made for unanticipated requirements and unforeseen problems. Both emphasize the

---

[148] Lovejoy, Ann. *The Handbook of Northwest Gardening* (Seattle: Sasquatch Books, 2003), Chapter 1.

[149] See *Growing Business Intelligence*, pp. 7-9.

importance of getting working products before customers as early as possible, to allow for the best possible feedback.

In Agile, as in Human-Centered Design, design patterns and existent solutions are encouraged, but teams need to understand where and how to apply creativity in response to particular needs and circumstances. In some cases, it may be necessary to find or create a new solution where an existent solution cannot be found (in the SCRUM methodology, this is called a "Spike").

In both approaches, the product must be owned by the customer. The customer's needs dictate solutions, and therefore, the customer feels a sense of ownership of the solution, thus ensuring that the solution will be used and will contribute value. Agile originally arose in response to failed IT projects where customers never used expensive software solutions created by IT.

Finally, both approaches emphasize progressive understanding of a problem and continual improvement of the problem-solving process. At each step of the process, we understand more about the problem we are trying to solve, and we become more adept in our approach to solving it.

THE MENTAL MATRIX

The processes of HCD involve iterations through several different types of thinking; no one approach to reasoning will take a person through a difficult problem. For example, HCD involves both *convergent* and *divergent* thinking,[150] where brainstorming is first used to create a set of possible solutions (*divergence*). Then those solutions are evaluated, tested, and narrowed down (*convergence*). Divergent thinking is a more creative and artistic process, while convergent thinking is more pragmatic and scientific.

---

[150] *Change by Design*, pp. 66-68.

Similarly, HCD involves both *analysis* and *synthesis* in its approach to problem-solving.[151] It is necessary to gather as much data as is needed (through interviewing stakeholders, for example). Then this data must be sifted through and analyzed to produce insights that suggest possible solution approaches. But at some point, the insights suggested by the data need to be woven together (i.e., *synthesized*) into some sort of coherent narrative about what problem is going to be addressed and how it is going to be solved. The analysis of the data is science; the crafting of the solution narrative is art. To quote Tim Brown[152]:

> *Sometimes the data are highly technical – if the task is a sophisticated piece of medical equipment, for instance. In other cases, they may be purely behavioral; for example, if the problem is to encourage people to switch to energy-saving compact fluorescent bulbs. In every case we may think of the designer as a master storyteller whose skill is measured by his or her ability to craft a compelling, consistent and believable narrative. It's no accident that writers and journalists now often work alongside mechanical engineers and cultural anthropologists on design teams.*

Design thinking is characterized by a tolerance for risk-taking and a willingness to experiment, to "think outside the box" in the search for effective solutions. Granted that organizations need to impose reasonable limits on both risk-taking and experimentation, they are most effective when the corporate culture supports the following conditions[153]:

- Everyone in the organization has the freedom to experiment (not just engineers and designers).

---

[151] Ibid, pp. 68-70.

[152] Ibid, p. 70.

[153] Ibid, pp. 73-74.

- Those people most exposed to changing externalities (e.g., new technologies, shifting markets and customer needs, strategic threats, and opportunities) are the ones who should lead the response.

- Ideas should not be favored based on who creates them (repeat aloud).

- Ideas that create a "buzz" (and gain vocal support within the organization) should receive organizational support.

- The "gardening skills" of senior leadership should direct the tending, pruning, and harvesting of ideas.

- An overarching purpose should be articulated so that the organization has a sense of direction and so that innovators don't feel the need for constant supervision.

The most important component of the HCD "Mental Matrix" is *optimism*; the unshakeable belief that things can be better than they are. To quote again from Tim Brown[154]:

To harvest the power of design thinking, individuals, teams, and whole organizations have to cultivate optimism. People have to believe that it is within their power (or at least the power of their team) to create new ideas that will serve unmet needs, and that will have a positive impact.

Optimism is the key to success because, as Tim Brown puts it, "curiosity does not thrive in organizations that have grown cynical."[155] Without optimism, people who are willing to take risks are driven out; new ideas are smothered before they

---

[154] Ibid, p. 76.

[155] Not to mention organizations in which initiative, free-thinking and risk-taking are discouraged or punished.

have a chance to come to life, and potential leaders leave the organization out of fear and uncertainty. Successful organizations foster a corporate culture of optimism and (reasonable) risk-taking and experimentation. This is another example of what I refer to as an "Agile Attitude"!

THE SEVEN MINDSETS OF HCD

Optimism is one of the "Seven Mindsets" of Human-Centered Design:

1. *Empathy*. The capacity to step into other people's shoes and understand their dilemmas. Designers must put themselves in the shoes of the people they are designing for and see the world through their eyes.

2. *Optimism*. A creative embracing of possibility and a belief in progress. Designers need to be focused on what can be achieved, not on the obstacles in the way.

3. *Iteration*. The design process must be nimble, iterative, and ongoing. With each iteration, we get closer to the end goal by prototyping, testing, and evaluating, as we get a better understanding of the problem to be solved.

4. *Creative Confidence*. The belief that we can and will come up with creative solutions to big problems.

5. *Making*. Make abstract ideas real by creating real-world prototypes that people can work with and provide feedback on.

6. *Embracing Ambiguity*. The proscription against trying to get to the "correct" answer too soon, an important aspect of HCD. Designers must be willing to explore alternative approaches and new ideas, even those that make them uncomfortable, and should be willing to

step outside their comfort zones to embrace new ways of doing things.

7. *Learning from Failure.* Failure guides design thinkers in their work; when they finally get it right, it's because they got it wrong first. The mantra "fail early to succeed sooner" is part of the HCD mindset.

The Seven Mindsets of Human-Centered Design are nicely summed up in this quote from *The Field Guide to Human-Centered Design*[156]:

> *Human-centered designers are unlike other problem solvers – we tinker and test, we fail early and often, and we spend a surprising amount of time not knowing the answer to the challenge at hand. And yet, we forge ahead. We're optimists and makers, experimenters and learners, we empathize and iterate, and we look for inspiration in unexpected places. We believe that a solution is out there and that by keeping focused on the people we're designing for and asking the right questions, we'll get there together. We dream up lots of ideas, some that work and some that don't. We make our ideas tangible so that we can test them, and then we refine them. In the end, our approach amounts to wild creativity, to a ceaseless push to innovate, and a confidence that leads us to solutions we'd never dreamed of when we started.*

THE PROCESS OF HCD

The process of Human-Centered Design encompasses three main phases:

1. *Inspiration.* In this phase, designers frame the design question, determine the scope of the problem and the target audience, and conduct interviews and group activities that enable them to see the problem from the point of view of those affected. The design team

---

[156] The Field Guide to Human-Centered Design (IDEA.org, 2016), p. 10.

also conducts the necessary research from secondary sources that will enable them to understand the problem.

2. *Ideation*. In this phase, designers use brainstorming to produce possible solutions to be explored and evaluated. The design team shares what they've learned from the previous phase, finds common themes and insights, and translates these insights into possible solutions by framing them as "How Might We..." questions.

3. *Implementation*. In this phase, a working prototype of a possible solution is built and tested, and given to the target audience for evaluation and feedback. Oftentimes, several different possible solutions are prototyped, tested, and evaluated at the same time to determine the best approach. Also, in this phase, the necessary partnerships are established that will be needed to bring the product to market.

These three phases are iterative, repeating over and over until a successful working solution has been built and is in the hands of the customers.

THE GOALS OF HCD

The goal of Human-Centered Design is to arrive at solutions that are *Desirable* (from a human standpoint), *Viable* (from a business standpoint), and *Feasible* (from a technology standpoint). The following graph shows the intersection of these three goals, which is where we can expect to find the optimal solution(s) to any given problem:

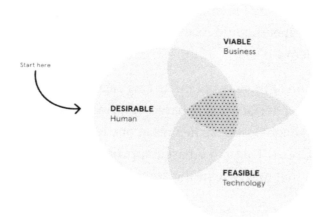

We start with what is needed (or desirable) from the point of view of the people for whom we are trying to solve the problem. Once we've determined a set of possible solutions that could appeal to the community we're trying to serve, then we refine this set of solutions down to what is both technologically feasible to implement and viable from a business/financial standpoint.

All three goals need to be achieved to have an acceptable solution to a given design problem.

EXAMPLES OF HUMAN-CENTERED DESIGN

We're going to see a wonderful example of the application of HCD to a data modeling problem in the next chapter (courtesy of my friend John Giles). For now, let's look at some more general examples of HCD in action:

- One of my favorite HCD stories involves a group of engineering students at the University of Washington who were asked by one of the Native American tribes to find out why their source of water had dried up. After several weeks of work with specialized instruments failed to find the cause of the problem, they asked the oldest surviving member of the tribe whether she remembered when the water system had been put in. She did. They asked her if she remembered the location of the water source.

She did, and directed them to the water source up in the mountains. From there, the engineers could locate the broken water pipe that was the cause of the problem.

- Duolingo, one of the most popular language learning apps, has a very simple-to-use interface that is based on principles of gaming. The user has to solve language-based challenges at one level before being allowed to move to the next. This game-based approach to learning alleviates the rote tedium that makes learning languages difficult.

- IDEO was asked by a medical device producer to design a device that nurses would use to enter data during medical procedures. The client had a vision of a sleek, futuristic gadget that the nurses would hold with two hands (picture how someone would hold an iPad) during the operation. But when the IDEO team watched the medical procedure take place, they noticed something that would make a two-handed device completely impossible. When patients were going into the operation, they were really nervous and afraid. So the first thing that almost every nurse did was hold the patient's hand to comfort them—an obvious human element their client hadn't noticed. IDEO went back to their office to brainstorm potential solutions, and they came up with a device that had a thumb scroll so nurses could do everything with one hand. That way they could input data and hold the patient's hand. It wasn't as "cool" as the client initially imagined, but it was much more human and practical.[157]

- In 1996, Oral-B asked IDEO to design a new toothbrush for kids. The first thing the IDEO team said was that they needed to watch kids brush their teeth. As you can probably imagine, the Oral-B executives thought this was a strange request. You want to go into people's homes—into their

---

[157] "IDEO's Human-Centered Design Process: How to Make Things People Love". UserTesting, December 4, 2018. https://bit.ly/3cHcnNz.

bathrooms—and watch their kids brush their teeth? Everyone already knows how people brush their teeth, is that really necessary?

As strange as it sounds, that's exactly what they did. They needed to see how kids *actually* brush their teeth, and they didn't want to make any assumptions. During their observations, they noticed that the way kids hold their toothbrushes is totally different than adults. Since adults have manual dexterity in their hands, they tend to use their fingers to manipulate the toothbrush with very fine movements. But kids just grab the toothbrush in their fist. The problem with adult toothbrushes was that they were hard for kids to hold. Since they were so small, they just flopped around in the kids' hands and were difficult to use.[158]

That one simple observation led to a new style of toothbrush: the squish gripper. And it totally innovated the kids-toothbrush space. If you go into any supermarket or corner store today, you'll notice kids' toothbrushes have fat, squishy handles. That's the power of observing the behavior of your users and integrating it into your design process.

- In 1894, W.K. Kellogg made a discovery that would forever change what we eat in the morning. Seeking a more digestible breakfast alternative to baked bread for his brother's hospital patients, the bespectacled former broom salesman accidentally left a pot of boiled wheat out overnight. The wheat became softened and when he rolled it out and baked it, each grain became a crispy flake. Kellogg tried the technique on corn. Over the course of several years, he perfected the tasty flakes by experimenting with different formulas and testing them with his brother's patients. He had invented — or designed — corn flakes.

But Kellogg didn't stop there. He believed that the entire population — not just hospital patients with special diet restrictions — would enjoy the

---

[158] Ibid.

new food, and he carefully positioned and marketed it. He created a recognizable brand and set about continually improving packaging that kept the product fresh. The product went on to sell 175,000 cases in its first year, laying the foundation for the $22.5 billion company that still bears Kellogg's name.

Kellogg's genius came not just in his flair for food product invention, but also in his customer-centric approach, iterative prototyping process, and careful consideration of the entire product experience — from the cereal itself to its packaging, marketing and distribution. Kellogg was more than a brilliant food scientist and marketer. He was also a brilliant designer.[159]

- Dementia and Alzheimer's are common among patients living at Lantern's assisted living facilities in Ohio. Jean Makesh, who heads up Lantern, has put together a five-part program that aims to prolong each stage of the diseases, thereby stalling the rate of degeneration in the brain.

  One of these parts is called Patient Environment. Here, the Patient Environment mimics the memory of living in an average suburb, whilst maintaining the safety of a secure facility. Almost like a set at Disneyland, the corridor accessing each room is actually a fake 'street' accessing each 'home.' Front porches, weatherboard cladding, street lights, planters, green carpet to represent grass — all of these are intended to trigger memories in the patients.

  "The design is meant, in part, to connect to Alzheimer's patients who often retain early memories from their first few decades of life, even as they slowly lose things from later years", says Makesh.[160]

---

[159]   Thomsen, Dave. "Why Human-Centered Design Matters". Wired.com, December 2013. https://bit.ly/3vrn3q1.

[160] Sughito, Esther. "Why Human-Centered Design Makes a Difference in Architecture". Medium.com, September 13, 2016. https://bit.ly/3xi7Kl0.

I could give a hundred more examples, but you get the idea. These are all examples of design that starts from observing human behavior and focusing on human needs. Design decisions are based on observation of how people actually do things, as opposed to how we *think* they do them (or should do them). Solutions are iteratively prototyped, and their impact on customers (and the problem we're trying to solve) evaluated. And the process of Human-Centered Design applies not only to the design of the product but to the entire process of creating, deploying, marketing, and supporting it.

Key Points

- Human-Centered Design (HCD) is an approach to practical problem-solving based on iterative implementations (i.e., prototyping) of design solutions developed in collaboration with the people most directly affected by the problem.

- There are close parallels between HCD and Agile. Both are collaborative and iterative processes in which creativity and experimentation are encouraged (within reasonable limits). Both acknowledge that all requirements cannot be determined ahead of time and that provision must be made for unanticipated requirements and unforeseen problems. Both emphasize the importance of getting working products before customers as early as possible to allow for the best possible feedback.

- HCD involves both *convergent* and *divergent* thinking. Brainstorming is first used to create a set of possible solutions (divergence), and then those solutions are evaluated, tested, and narrowed down (convergence).

- HCD involves both analysis and synthesis in its approach to problem-solving. Data is gathered and analyzed, and then the resulting insights are woven together to create a coherent narrative about the problem and its solution.

- The Seven Mindsets of HCD are: Empathy, Optimism, Iteration, Creative Confidence, Making, Embracing Ambiguity, and Learning from Failure.

- The three main phases of the HCD process are inspiration (framing the question), ideation (brainstorming the solution), and implementation (prototyping the solution and getting customer feedback).

- The goal of Human-Centered Design is to arrive at solutions that are desirable (from a human standpoint), viable (from a business standpoint), and feasible (from a technology standpoint).

Chapter 20
Data Modeling and Design

The customer's perception is your reality.

Kate Zabriskie

At this point, let's go back to the question of whether data modeling can (or cannot) be considered a design activity (as opposed to merely a descriptive activity). You'll remember we suggested a few reasons that data modeling might be considered a design activity:

- If what we are modeling is not reality itself, but the way in which *information about reality* is perceived and processed by people, then the modeling process is likely to involve the creation of new constructs. Data modelers often talk about "modeling the business", but what is actually modeled are people's perceptions about how the business works.

- The process of data modeling can elicit information about user requirements that might not be surfaced otherwise, since traditional user stories only surface functional requirements, not data requirements.

- Data models can suggest opportunities for creating new data entities that don't currently exist.

- Data models can be useful when examining and improving current business processes.

- Data models can also drive useful conversations about business processes that don't exist yet or are still being formulated.

This means that data models can be more than just descriptions of existing data entities and business processes. The data modeling process can result in the creation of new data entities and improved business processes.

However, the question is: how can we use data models in ways that mesh with design thinking? How can we do data modeling in a way that is creative, and not merely descriptive?

DESIGN THINKING AND DATA MODELING

So how do the principles of design thinking guide us in thinking about data modeling (and other data work), and specifically, about the extent to which data modeling is a creative (i.e., design) process?

1) Data modeling should properly be done from the very beginning of a project, and data modelers should be involved in the gathering and elaboration of requirements. Often, data modelers aren't brought aboard until after the use cases have been created, but I have found that data modelers can ask questions during requirements-gathering sessions that other people don't think of, and they can surface information about business requirements that otherwise wouldn't be known. At my company, even developers agree that a fuller understanding of business requirements and the problem domain results when data modelers, business analysts (or subject-matter experts), and application analysts work together to understand the business problem and elaborate the

requirements. We have already noted that use cases, by themselves, do not adequately capture data requirements or important information about the business data domain.

2) The focus of data modeling should not be on merely understanding and supporting existing business processes. Rather, we should be looking to understand how these processes could be improved and asking whether we are currently doing the best thing that could be done. When I was in school, I remember being asked to create a data model for a video rental store. It didn't occur to me then to ask whether supporting this particular business model was a good idea.

3) Data modeling (and other data work) must be iterative in execution and provide for the reality that we won't fully understand the problem to be solved until we try to solve it. We must also understand that, in solving the problem, new problems will surface that will need to be solved.

4) Data modelers should make judicious use of past solutions (e.g., data model patterns and existing data models), but should make sure the pattern(s) used are a good fit for the problem that is being solved. At the same time, data modelers need to be flexible and open to the possible need to modify the pattern(s) to better fit the problem that is being solved.

5) Data modeling should be done in such a way that the data model produced can be used to solve future problems in that domain space. This is why previous chapters have mentioned the importance of drawing from and adding to canonical and enterprise data models in domain modeling.

6) A data model shouldn't be thought of as a one-way transfer of information from the mind of the data modeler to the project team. That is, as a definitive statement of business data requirements. Rather, the

data model should support a design process known as *conjecture-analysis*, in which requirements emerge through client feedback on proposed designs.[161] The data model should be a *living document* reflecting the current understanding of the requirements and the design of the proposed solution, as agreed to by all the project stakeholders. As Graeme Simsion notes, "a good data model is one which creates a shared understanding, and the way to develop such a model is through participation and facilitation".[162]

7) The worth of a data model is not determined by the extent to which it fits prescribed norms of what a data model should look like or how it should be produced. The worth of a data model is determined by the extent to which it can support the process of bringing people together to solve a problem or achieve a goal. The process of creating the data model should never interfere with or impede the process of solving the problem or achieving the goal.

8) The amount of data modeling required in any given phase of a project is determined by the goals of that phase (e.g., sprint goals in an Agile project) and the amount of information needed by the project stakeholders to meet those goals. Be wary of modeling too far in advance of requirements or project needs, especially when doing so may adversely impact the project schedule.

9) When modeling, keep the "big picture" in mind. Understand the current state of the business, the desired "to be" state, and the business processes and stakeholders that need to be supported.

---

[161] Simsion, p. 65, from Roozenburg, N. F. M. and N. G. Cross (1991). "Models of the Design Process: Integrating Across the Disciplines". *Design Studies* 12(4): 215-220.

[162] Simsion, p. 65, from De Carteret, C. and R. Vidgen (1995). *Data Modeling for Information Systems* (London, UK: Pitman Publishing), p. 368.

10) People skills (i.e., facilitation and other "soft skills") are as important to data modeling as technical or analytical skills. A good data modeler will use a data model as a tool to bring the expertise of others to bear on finding the solution to a problem.

11) Data modelers also need to be able to find creative solutions to problems as they arise. For example, I once needed to define a Chassis (truck) entity in a data model. However, the attributes of a Chassis could not be predefined; engineers needed the ability to add new Chassis attributes at will without having to change the schema of the Chassis table. So, I adapted a data model pattern[163] to the problem and came up with the following solution:

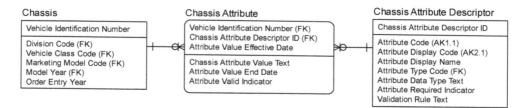

To add a new attribute to a Chassis, one need only add a record to the Chassis Attribute Descriptor table, specifying an attribute code, name, type, datatype, nullability indicator, and regex validation rule. The Chassis Attribute table provides the mapping between a specific Chassis and all of its related attributes. Note that the Chassis Attributes have effective date ranges, so attributes can be removed from a Chassis as well as added. A view in the database provides applications with a pivot (table) view of a Chassis and its attributes. The regex validation rule is used to ensure that the value of the attribute in Chassis Attribute Value Text matches the business definition of the attribute; a daily report is sent to the Engineering Division alerting them to data values that do not fit the defined validation rules.

---

[163] David Hay calls this the "Specification" pattern, while Len Silverston calls it the "Product Feature" pattern.

HCD and Data Modeling

Now, how do we apply the concepts of Human-Centered Design to data modeling and other data work? This question isn't intuitively obvious; data modeling and database development are not tasks we instinctively think of as wildly creative and experimental endeavors! For example, applying HCD to data modeling requires that we change our whole understanding of what a data model is and how to produce it. We need to think of a data model as not just a static depiction of an organization's data assets but as the *design of a solution* to one or more specific business problems. Once we view data modeling in these terms, we can apply an HCD design approach to it.

INSPIRATION

As mentioned early on, one of the most important reasons for doing data modeling is to bring people together to a shared understanding of the data-related aspects of a particular business problem or goal, and to forge agreement on the data-related solution(s) to that problem. The data modeler must put himself or herself into the customer's shoes, see the problem through their eyes, and feel their pain. The data modeler needs to talk with stakeholders to understand the business problem fully, and do the necessary secondary research to understand its business context. The data modeler needs to be involved in a project from its inception, to help guide (and understand) conversations around the goal(s) of the project, the affected stakeholders, and the scope of the problem to be solved. Other project stakeholders (e.g., the project manager) may not understand or fully appreciate the data aspects of a business problem or business need; this is where the expertise of a data practitioner can be most valuable.

IDEATION

Once the business problem is understood, the data modeler can then, through the process of facilitation, bring group collaboration and consensus to the identifying of possible design solutions. With the data modeler's guidance, design patterns that have been used for similar problems in the past can be evaluated and discussed. Possible data model designs can be whiteboarded (or drawn in a modeling tool and shared via collaboration software) and discussed. Alternative approaches can be proposed, discussed, and voted on. Design solutions can be "prototyped" using spreadsheets with sample data (or schema definitions with sample XML or JSON documents) and evaluated. Sticky notes on a whiteboard or wall can be used to "brainstorm" data entities, attributes, and relationships.

IMPLEMENTATION

Once an iteration of the logical data model has been agreed upon (remember, this is an iterative process), the data modeler will meet with the application development team (the implementation stakeholders) to discuss the best approach for physically instantiating and persisting data in a form that can easily be consumed and manipulated by the application (or service). As previously stated, the objective is to ensure that data is not persisted or represented in ways that violate the business' understanding of the data definitions or data properties. Within these parameters, an appropriate choice of architecture and technology can be made, and an acceptable physical data design created. Help may also be needed to populate the data structures (perhaps migrated from existing data sources), and the data practitioner can advise the development team on the most effective ways of consuming, updating, and integrating the data.

Data professionals should always remember the Three Goals of HCD: Solutions that are desirable from a human point of view (i.e., that actually address the problem that needs to be solved for our customers), feasible from a technology point of view (i.e., that can be quickly and easily implemented, and are robust, scalable and performant), and viable from a business point of view (i.e., are cost-justifiable for the business, and deliver business value in excess of their cost). All data solutions, including data models and physical databases (or data stores), need to meet these three criteria.

John Giles has a great story about this, based on the work of Australian data modeler Graham Witt:

A mining company had a problem. They had expensive machinery, and when it broke, the cost of downtime at the mine could be huge. Too often, a part was ordered, but when it eventually arrived, it was found to be the wrong part. The cycle went back to reordering, hopefully for the right part.

Someone had a brainwave. You've probably seen "explosion diagrams" for common household products such as lawn mowers. In one diagram, you can see all the parts and where they fit together. The idea was to create explosion diagrams for the mine's machinery, with touch screens located across the entire mine site, so that a person could point at a diagram, identify the faulty part, and generate an order. Possibly a really good IT solution, but expensive and a massive undertaking, especially getting engineers and technical drawing experts to create the explosion diagrams.

Graham visited the site, and worked hard to get familiarity. He pulled several observations together. The first was that a small number of old-timers in the parts store had collective experience spanning decades. They knew the machines, they knew the parts. If they could be involved in the ordering process, the likelihood of incorrect orders pretty well disappeared. The next observation was that almost all mine vehicles were equipped with CB radios.

The solution? Roster the core team of old-timer store people so that at least one of them is always on duty. Then dedicate one of the spare CB channels to be the "parts" channel. If anyone in the field has a problem, they jump on the CB radio, and talk directly to the central store expert who will probe, ask for more details, and make a decision on the parts to be ordered.

The result? Consistent ordering of the correct parts, with zero outlay on new equipment and zero delay in implementation. The only possible loser might have been the IT company who was no longer required!

In this case, the best design solution was simply to tap into the expertise of experienced people and empower them to do their jobs. This is one of the fundamental principles of both HCD *and* Agile!

Key Points

- To do data modeling in a design way, data modelers must help shape requirements, guide understanding of the problem to be solved, help improve existing processes, deliver reusable solutions, and support iterative customer feedback.

- The worth of a data model is not determined by the extent to which it fits prescribed norms of what a data model should look like or how it should be produced. The worth of a data model is determined by the extent to which it can support the process of bringing people together to solve a problem or achieve a goal.

- Creating the data model should never interfere with or impede the process of solving the problem or achieving the goal.

- The process of data modeling involves both surfacing problems that may not have been recognized and finding creative solutions for them.

- As with HCD, data modeling involves the processes of *Inspiration, Ideation,* and *Implementation*.

- A data model should always reflect the Three Goals of HCD: solutions that are desirable from a human point of view (i.e., that actually address the problem that needs to be solved for our customers), feasible from a technology point of view (i.e., that can be quickly and easily implemented, and are robust, scalable and performant), and viable from a business point of view (i.e., are cost-justifiable for the business, and deliver business value in excess of their cost).

Section V
Case Study

If you're not prepared to be wrong, you'll never come up with anything original.

Ken Robinson

To illustrate the application of the concepts in this book, I'm going to continue the saga of a fictional company called "Blue Moon Guitar Company".[164] The company designs and builds custom guitars and other wooden stringed instruments to order. When ordering an instrument, the customer can specify several customization options, such as size, finish, type of wood used, and more. Each model of instrument is associated with a set of these customization options, and each option specified contributes to the total list price of the instrument.

The company has different manufacturing divisions, each of which makes instruments under a particular brand name. The divisions are more or less autonomous and are allowed to set their own prices. Each division has its own factories, and costs of parts (components of each instrument) and labor (for

---

[164] I created this fictional company as the Case Study in my first book, *Building the Agile Database*.

assembly) vary for each factory. Parts and labor cost data for each factory is maintained in databases on the company's central mainframe computer.

Pricing managers at each division input and manage the customization options for each model of instrument made by that division. Each option/model combination can be associated with an assembly of parts (either individual parts or part structures) called a *configuration*. The aggregate of parts and labor data for each configuration is factored into a set of calculations that determines the base price of the instrument before any discounting is applied. Option, option/model, configuration, and pricing data is kept separate by division. The data for a division can only be viewed and updated by that division's pricing managers.

Each model of instrument has a standard configuration, consisting of a set of standard options. Each standard option is associated with a standard assembly of parts; these assemblies can be shared by more than one standard option. Options are added to or removed from the standard configuration to create a custom instrument.

Blue Moon also has a subsidiary division that sells aftermarket replacement parts to customers and guitar shops worldwide.

THE PROJECT

Blue Moon decided to revamp its product registration, warranty, and warranty claims business processes. To this end, they purchased a software package that allows companies to customize the software to fit their particular business processes. The software allows the user to define business workflows, along with the data that supports those workflows. The software runs on an Oracle database.

I was tasked with doing the data modeling for the project. Since most of the application functionality was going to be "out of the box", with only a limited amount of customization, I estimated 350 hours for the modeling work. Our

Oracle DBA estimated 250 hours for the database support. We looked back on this later and laughed over several drinks. We had no idea what was coming.

At this point, the Warranty project was just one of several projects I was supporting. I got a foreshadowing of what was to come when I was told to move my desk into the work area occupied by the Warranty project team. Why, I asked. Simple: I was being assigned to the project "full time" (minus the time I had to spend on all my other projects). Why? Because I was also going to be doing all of the database development, stored procedure coding, data migration and integration, data quality assessment, etc.

This was going to be an Agile project, but with a twist. There were going to be *three* teams, one on-site and two offshore. Each team had its own scrum master, the project, itself, had a separate dedicated scrum master, project manager, product owner, and director. I was supporting all three project teams.

You'll recall from *Building the Agile Database* that Agile presents a problem for people in enterprise-focused positions who have to support several different projects at the same time and who can't be 100% dedicated to a single project. Moreover, I am also our company's data and BI architect, as well as its only data modeler. Now, on this one project, I had to support not one Agile team, but three!

You'll also recall that my solution to this problem involves finding what I call *Allies* and *Surrogates*. *Allies* are people (usually but not always in management) who can clear away roadblocks, acquire resources, resolve conflicts with other managers, and so on. *Surrogates* are people you can push some of your work onto to give you time to do other things. I was going to need both.

My first step was to go to one of our directors and get myself relieved of as many of my other responsibilities as possible. In the end, I had this project and maybe two others to support. The director sent the word down that nobody was to ask me for anything without his approval.

My second step was to look for people who could help me. Fortunately, I found a friend right away in the Lead System Architect (LSA) for the project, a contractor who I'll call Mukesh. Mukesh is highly skilled, intelligent, personable, and experienced. He has done several projects involving the software we have purchased and knows it inside and out. He is also very knowledgeable in matters of data. Although his practical database skills are a bit limited, he knows how to talk to business users about database requirements. Mukesh and the BAs (Business Analysts) did the initial requirements-gathering sessions with the business. Mukesh then reviewed the requirements with me, and I either gave him questions to take back to the business or scheduled follow-up sessions so I could talk to the business users directly.

I also got a lot of help from another contractor, who I'll call Sridevi. She had a lot of database experience, including SQL and stored procedure coding, and came in very handy during the actual database development work.

It's a good thing that I'm good at making friends, because this project quickly mushroomed out of control, and I needed all the friends I could find.

Another note: In situations where you are (or might become) overloaded, it's very important to be transparent about what's happening. Make sure everyone (including your project leader and your manager) knows what you're working on at all times, and are aware of who is asking you for what. They can help prioritize your workload and keep unimportant things off your plate.

DATA MODELING CHALLENGES

I don't know whether anybody's written about this, but I'll say it now: the most important skill a data modeler can possess is the ability to negotiate. Over the course of the next several months, I had to negotiate more deals than Donald Trump. This is, of course, one of the central tenets of Agile: you have to be willing and able to negotiate deals that allow the project to continue on track, rather than "sticking to your guns" and allowing the project to flounder. As I said in *Building the Agile Database*, you don't want to "win the battles" and yet lose the war (i.e., have the project fail with your name on it)!

I've already previously alluded to one of these challenges: the software's use of delegated tables. Since these tables are defined and maintained by application users, and correspond to application screens, I had to fight to get them defined in a reasonable way. The one point I had to concede was allowing "non-normalized" data to be included in the table definition for the convenience (i.e., reference) of the business users maintaining the table. For these delegated tables, I used a colored fill to denote the table as delegated, I used a colored font to indicate the redundant attributes (which are defined in the data model as physical-only), and I used a comment box for explanations, as required:

The application's use of delegated tables ended up derailing some of my early data modeling efforts on the project. For example, I originally modeled a set of Contact tables to store Contact Names, Addresses, Phone Numbers, etc. I had intended to use these tables to store Customer, Dealer, and Supplier data (as separate Contact Types). However, we ended up using these tables only for Customer data during the Product Registration process, as this data was the only data actually entered through the application. As it turned out, the Dealer and Supplier data for the application was managed using delegated tables.

Modeling the Dealer data turned out to be more complicated than I anticipated. Not only couldn't I use the Contact tables I'd modeled, I ended up having to model two separate tables for Dealer data because this data was maintained by two separate business units in two different places. Data involving the grouping of Dealers into Dealer Groups and Owner Groups was maintained by our Dealer Development group. Data involving the grouping of Dealers into Sales Regions and Service Regions was maintained by our Sales and Marketing group. We imported the Dealer Development data into a table called *Dealer Hierarchy* from their application database nightly. We uploaded the Sales and Marketing data from a spreadsheet into a delegated table called *Dealer Information*. At the time, we had no MDM solution (we're working on one now), so there was no centralized repository of Dealer data to draw from. I was, however, able to refer to other company data models that included the Dealer entity.

Resolving these issues involved several sessions of Mukesh, me, and our business users standing at a whiteboard, writing out sample data, and drawing, erasing, and re-drawing suggestions for the table schemas. There were also negotiations (some protracted) over which business group would be allowed to manage which set of data. What started out as a simple data modeling exercise turned out to be an excursion into data governance!

The next modeling challenge was the *Product* table. Mukesh insisted that the Product table be keyed on Product Serial Number, which would apply not only to our warrantied products but also to warrantied parts. The problem, we discovered, is that some of our product codes contain embedded "intelligence" (i.e., "intelligent keys"), and that these product codes sometimes need to be changed. We also discovered that our legacy Warranty Claims data often had missing or incomplete product codes, which couldn't be loaded into the new system. It required some management assistance to reach the following resolution:

- An edict from senior management that product codes would not be changed once a product was entered into the system via product registration or warranty registration.

- Only products with current warranty registrations would be imported into the new system. Legacy warranties and warranty claims would be exported from our mainframe computer into an Operational Data Store (ODS). The new application would be given a feature where users could search for legacy warranties based on partial product codes and other product data, and an API would search the ODS for matches based on the user input.

- In the event that products with duplicate or partially-missing product codes needed to be imported into the application, other product-related data (such as manufacturing division, model year or product make/model) would be appended to the serial number to create a unique value. I added a comment to this effect next to the *Product* table in the data model.

- Questions around matching legacy warranty claims to products and warranties would be resolved by our Warranty Claims group.

One of the processes that needed to be supported by the application was Recall Campaigns (product recalls due to defects discovered after production). A consequence of not having all the Product data available in the application was that we were still obligated to process Recall Campaigns for legacy products that were not in the database. That meant we could not enforce a foreign key (FK) constraint between a Recall Campaign and a Product in the database. I noted this in the data model by making the FK constraint logical-only and adding an explanatory comment as to why this was done.

One challenge I faced was mapping our company's business terms to the vernacular used by the software manufacturer. In some cases, it was like translating between two different languages using an interpreter! For example, we had to fit our Product Model data into an application table called *Product Master*:

Product Master

Category = Make (Mfr) Family = Model Class Series = Base Model Product = Sub-Model Model Code is Division+Sub-Model Option Code (for uniqueness).	Model Code: NOT NULL Category Code: NULL Category Description: NULL Family Code: NULL Family Description: NULL Series Code: NULL Series Description: NULL Model Description: NOT NULL

The comment box to the left of the table provides the translation between our business terminology (Model Class, Base Model, Sub-Model) and the terms used by the application (Category, Family, Series).

As the project went along, the data model became larger and more unwieldy. Fortunately, my modeling tool allowed me to create a single subject area for the domain (which we referred to as Next Generation Warranty, or NGW), and separate diagrams for the various sub-domains (Product Registration, Warranty, Warranty Claims, etc.). The advantage of doing this in the modeling tool is that I could copy entities from one sub-domain into another for reference purposes, and to show relationships. So I was really doing domain modeling, even though all of the sub-domains were being implemented in a single database. In this case, the database wasn't supporting multiple applications; it supported a single application that performed multiple business processes. The modeling tool helped me to ensure consistent entity and attribute definitions across the multiple sub-domains for the entire project. I also took advantage of the opportunity to update our Canonical data model with new attributes for Customer and Dealer.

Another challenge was the General Ledger (G/L) Account table. This table maps data attributes such as Division, Claim Category, Coverage Type, Country, and Responsibility Code to a set of accounting codes used to charge claims (or portions of claims) against a Dealer or a Supplier. Unfortunately, it took some time to determine the exact set of data attributes that could be used to determine an account code, and these attributes were in constant flux. Moreover, for any given record in the table, one or more of these attributes could be null. So, even though I have a natural (*sic*) aversion to surrogate keys, I was forced to use one for this table and then define an Alternate Key (AK), or unique index, for the six data attributes used to find the account codes:

G_L_ACCOUNT

G_L_ACCOUNT_ID: INTEGER NOT NULL
DIVISION_CODE: CHARACTER(1) NOT NULL (FK) (AK1.1) CLAIM_CATEGORY_CODE: VARCHAR2(4) NOT NULL (FK) (AK1.2) DEALER_DIVISION_CODE: CHAR(1) NOT NULL (AK1.3) DEALER_COUNTRY_CODE: CHAR(2) NOT NULL (FK) (AK1.4) RESPONSIBILITY_CODE: VARCHAR2(10) NULL (FK) (AK1.5) RESPONSIBILITY_DESC: VARCHAR2(255) NULL COVERAGE_TYPE_CODE: VARCHAR2(10) NULL (FK) (AK1.6) COVERAGE_TYPE_DESC: VARCHAR2(255) NULL DEALER_PAYMENT_ACCOUNT_CODE: VARCHAR2(25) NULL SUPPLIER_RECOVERY_ACCOUNT_CODE: VARCHAR2(25) NULL G_L_ACCOUNT_DESC: VARCHAR2(50) NULL

Responsibility Description and Coverage Type Description added to table for the convenience of the business.

Note that this, too, is a delegated table and that it has been denormalized to an extent by adding the description attributes from the Coverage Type and Responsibility tables for the convenience of the business users. I've added an explanatory comment to the table in the data model.

Finally, I'll explain the modeling of the Operation table, as this table will make an appearance later. An "operation" is an action that is performed during the repair of a product, such as replacing a particular part. This table defines a hierarchy of operations that match to product model groups. For each product model group and operation, there is a standard number of hours value that determines the labor cost for performing this action. The sum of the hours for all operations (actions) performed during the repair determines the labor cost associated with the warranty claim.

There are two things of note about the Operation table: the first is that, although it has a four-part natural key, only two attributes are needed to ensure uniqueness. The business insisted on the four-part key, since that was the way they were used to seeing the data in the legacy application. So I added an Alternate Key (AK) inside the Primary Key (PK), along with an explanatory note, to document the two attributes that actually needed to be unique.

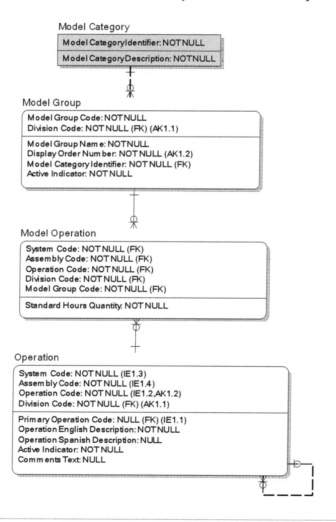

Figure 9: Data Model for Warranty Operations.

The other thing you'll notice are the separate English and Spanish description attributes. I pushed back some on this, as we already have a standard data modeling and database solution for supporting text in multiple languages. But Mukesh didn't want the complexity of that solution, and since we were able to establish that only two languages needed to be supported, and only in this one table, I didn't press the point.

DATABASE IMPLEMENTATION CHALLENGES

The main reason I was assigned to this project "full time" was that the contractors assigned to the project (for the most part) didn't have a lot of database development expertise. The need for this became more and more apparent as the project went along, growing from a single DBMS (Oracle) to a second (Teradata), a third (SQL Server), and a fourth (Snowflake). I ended up doing data modeling and database development work in all four database environments!

As already noted, the Oracle database contained both tables used natively by the software product, and custom tables that I modeled to hold our company's product, customer, dealer, warranty, campaign, and warranty claims data. The Teradata database was our Operational Data Store (ODS), holding legacy data exported from our mainframe and accessed mostly via APIs called by the application. Data from the Oracle databases was also exported nightly to the ODS, and the combined data was pipelined nightly to a Snowflake database in the Cloud that our business users access for organizational reporting and analytics. The SQL Server database was a specialized reporting database used by our Sales and Marketing people for product registration reporting. All four of these database implementations presented their own sets of challenges during the project.

Without getting too much into the technical aspects of the database solutions, there are a few aspects of the database implementation that should be mentioned:

First, I had to write several stored procedures in the Oracle database to support application processes. As you will remember from the section on Domain-Driven Development, a lot of developers don't like to have business (or application) logic stored in the database. But in this case, it was unavoidable; the data-intensive processing required could not be done by the application in a way that ensured adequate performance for the user. As I've explained in *Building the Agile Database*, it's a good idea to "let the database do the data work", and make use of the DBMS's resources and the Query Optimizer to perform data-intensive processing on the database server, and return only the results that are needed to the application.[165] Among the stored procedures I wrote to support the application were a procedure to determine the applicable warranties that could be offered for a given Product at registration time and a procedure to determine which warranties could be applied to a particular warranty claim, based on the type of claim, the part or parts affected, the particular product model, etc. This sort of processing is quick and easy to do in SQL; it is much harder (and time-consuming and resource-intensive) to do in Java.

One requirement that surfaced during the project was the need to capture (i.e., audit) changes made to various data values and create audit records of who changed the record and when, the PK values of the record, the before and after values of the data, etc. Fortunately, I had already created a trigger-based solution for this in SQL Server, and was able (with some difficulty) to port it to Oracle. The audit records generated from the triggers were written to a set of audit

---

[165] One important thing to note: we were using on-prem servers for this project, so we didn't have the sort of scalability we would have had in a cloud environment. However, as I'm constantly pointing out to people, even with cloud-based scalability you still have to pay for the resources you use. Ignoring good application and database design in the cloud makes sense only if you don't care how much money you have to spend.

tables, and a view was created to allow users and developers to query the data however they wanted.

I used triggers for other purposes as well; for example, to enforce complex data validation rules such as requiring certain data fields to have non-null values for a particular type or model of Product.

I also made extensive use of views in the database for the purpose of smoothing the mapping of database tables to screens in the application (that is, resolving the so-called "object-relational impedance mismatch"). This is an example of the "Virtual Data Layer" (or VDL) explained in *Building the Agile Database*; the database virtualization abstracts the data needed by the application in a way that masks the complexity of the underlying database schema.

In the case of the operation data described above, the application needed to see the data in a spreadsheet-style layout, with a row for each Operation record and columns for each Product Model Group. At the intersection of each Operation and Model Group would be the Standard Hours (labor) value. Those of you familiar with SQL will recognize this as a SQL Pivot Query, which can be done in a view. It was easy for the application to select from the view to bring the Operation data, in the correct form, directly into the application screen to display to the user.

However, for reporting outside the application, the business users wanted the view to return the product model descriptions in the column headings, not the product model codes. This can't be done dynamically in a SQL Pivot Query (unfortunately). The column header values have to be hard-coded in the query. So, I wrote a stored procedure that reads the Model Group table and generates the complete set of pivot views (both with codes in the column headers and with descriptions in the column headers). This way, whenever changes or additions are made to Model Groups, the stored procedure can be used to quickly and easily regenerate the pivot views of the Operation data.

LESSONS LEARNED

The principal "takeaway" that I want everyone to get from this story is that, whenever a problem or an obstacle occurred, I was able to work with other members of the project team to find a creative solution and implement it quickly enough to keep the project on track, and to meet our sprint goals and project timelines. As I've said many times, Agile is not so much a methodology as it is a mindset. So long as team members have a "can do", customer-service mindset and a positive attitude, almost anything can be achieved, and most obstacles overcome. This is what I've referred to as "having an Agile Attitude". And the importance of finding (or grooming) allies or surrogates, especially in a large and complex Agile project, cannot be over-emphasized. Our teams had to work hard to communicate and work together effectively, but they rose to the challenge and succeeded!

The size and complexity of this project enabled me to learn a lot of lessons about Domain modeling, and the breadth of the application also enabled me to complete a number of canonical data models for our organization (e.g., Product, Dealer and Customer). This work will pay dividends as we move forward into our Master Data Management and Data Governance initiatives.

One of the operative principles of Agile, that I don't think I've emphasized enough in my books, is that Agile projects succeed only if everybody assumes that everybody else is well-meaning; that everybody is doing their best to do the best possible job and ensure the success of the project. I saw this principle being lived out every single day of our project, and I attribute a lot of the success of the project to this shared sense of purpose and dedication. Despite occasional conflicts and communication difficulties, the sense of mutual respect for each other's professionalism never wavered, and was the glue that held the project team together.

In the end, each member of the team told their separate stories, and made their separate contributions, and the result was that the story of the new NGW application was told, and will continue to be told for a very long time to come.

Key Points

- To work effectively on Agile projects, it is often necessary to find *Allies* and *Surrogates*. *Allies* are people who can clear away roadblocks, acquire resources, resolve conflicts with other managers, and so on. *Surrogates* are people you can push some of your work onto to give you time to do other things.

- In situations where you are (or might become) overloaded, it's very important to be transparent about what's happening. Make sure everyone (including your project leader and your manager) know what you're working on at all times and are aware of who is asking you for what.

- The most important skill a data modeler can possess is the ability to negotiate. This is, of course, one of the central tenets of Agile: you have to be willing and able to negotiate deals that allow the project to continue on track, rather than "sticking to your guns" and allowing the project to founder.

- Use the resources available in the DBMS (including the query optimizer) to improve the performance and scalability of your application by "letting the database do the data work". Perform data-intensive processing on the database server, and return only the results needed to the application.

- Data virtualization, especially the use of views and table-valued functions, enable applications and business users to have the view of the data they want to see without having to deal with the underlying complexity of the database schema.

- Agile is not so much a methodology as it is a mindset. So long as team members have a "can do" customer-service mindset, and a positive attitude, almost anything can be achieved and most obstacles overcome. This is referred to as "having an Agile Attitude".

- Agile projects succeed only if everybody assumes that everybody else is well-meaning; that everybody is doing their best to do the best possible job and ensure the success of the project.

This will probably be the last data management book I will write. I will be retiring this year and plan to devote myself to more creative forms of writing, along with occasional lecturing and teaching. I've enjoyed my career in data management, and especially all the wonderful people I've had the privilege of meeting and working with over the years. I'd like to extend my special thanks and appreciation to Steve Hoberman for publishing, supporting, and promoting my books, and to Robert Seiner of TDAN (The Data Administration Newsletter), for supporting me in my early days and publishing my Agile data columns for so many years. Ditto to the Puget Sound Chapter of DAMA International, who have given me much support and comradery over the years.

And, of course, I will always be grateful to my friends and colleagues at our IT organization, who have nurtured me along from a fledgling DBA to a mature (more-or-less) data architect. I will always remember all of you fondly, and I enjoyed working with you all more than you will ever know. We've had a great run together.

Life goes on, and my greatest hope is that the books I've written will inspire others to find solutions to the problems they face and will then empower them to help others solve their own problems. As I've said often before, my books aren't intended to be prescriptive ("You must do everything my way!"), but rather are intended to be instructive and inspirational, helping my readers to find their own path through the swamp.

Keep an "Agile Attitude" and focus on making the world better for as many people as possible.

As always, I wish you continuing success on your journey.

Larry Burns has worked in IT for more than 40 years as a database developer, DBA, data modeler, application developer, consultant, and teacher. He holds a B.S. in Mathematics from the University of Washington, and a Master's degree in Software Engineering from Seattle University. He currently works for a global Fortune 200 company as a Data and BI Architect and Data Engineer (i.e., data modeler).

He contributed material on Database Development and Database Operations Management to the first edition of DAMA International's Data Management Body of Knowledge (DAMA-DMBOK), and is a former instructor and advisor in the certificate program for Data Resource Management at the University of Washington in Seattle. He has written numerous articles for TDAN.com and DMReview.com, and is the author of *Building the Agile Database* (Technics Publications LLC, 2011) and *Growing Business Intelligence* (Technics Publications LLC, 2016).

His interests include music, gardening, writing, and landscaping.

He lives in Kent, Washington with his wife Becky.

Agile Alliance. A wealth of information about Agile development, its philosophy, and best practices can be found on the website of the Agile Alliance at www.agilealliance.org.

Agile Data. Information about traditional approaches to Agile data development can be found at www.agiledata.org.

Business Process Reengineering. The best books on this subject are *Reengineering the Corporation* by Michael Hammer and James Champy, and *Beyond Reengineering* by Michael Hammer. Thomas Davenport is another author who has contributed significantly in this area.

COMN. For anyone interested in learning more about the Common and Object Modeling Notation, there are a number of good articles on the TDAN (www.tdan.com) and Dataversity (www.dataversity.net) websites. I can also recommend the book *NoSQL and SQL Data Modeling* by Ted Hills (Technics Publications LLC).

DAMA International. DAMA International is the recognized source for education, certification, and information regarding best practices in the data management profession. Information about DAMA can be found on their website at www.dama.org.

DAMA DMBOK. DAMA International's Data Management Body of Knowledge (DMBOK) is a compendium of standards and industry best practices for the management of data as an enterprise asset. Copies of the DMBOK (in print, PDF or CD-ROM) can be obtained from Technics Publications.

Domain-Driven Design. The most useful information I've seen on this subject comes from articles written by Martin Fowler. Most of these are available on his website (www.martinfowler.com). I can also recommend the book *Domain-Driven Design* by Eric Evans.

Fact-Based Modeling. The book *Object-Role Modeling Fundamentals* by Terry Halpin is an excellent introduction to ORM, from one of its foremost practitioners. His book takes the reader step-by-step through the process of creating ORM models.

A lot of my inspiration for the concept of "Working Toward" and similar design concepts comes from Ann Lovejoy's *Handbook of Northwest Gardening,* one of the best books ever written on the art of gardening and landscape design. I recommend it to anyone with an interest in landscape gardening, even if you don't live in the Northwest.

Graph Data Modeling. Thomas Frisendal's book *Graph Data Modeling for NoSQL and SQL* is one of the best reference works in this area. He also draws a lot of inspiration for his data modeling work from the field of Cognitive Psychology, which means that he concerns himself with the Why of data modeling as well as the How. His book is useful not only for practitioners of Graph Modeling, but for all data modeling practitioners as well.

Human-Centered Design. IDEO has a number of resources for Human-Centered design available on their website (www.ideo.org), including *The Field Guide to Human-Centered Design*. The website also contains numerous examples of the work they are doing, especially in Third-World countries. I can also recommend the books *Change by Design* by Tim Brown, and two books by Jeanne Liedtka: *Designing for Growth* and *Solving Problems with Design Thinking*. I can also recommend two books by Don Norman: *The Design of Everyday Things* and *Emotional Design: Why We Love (Or Hate) Everyday Things*. Norman does a wonderful job of presenting essential design concepts as fascinating stories from real-world experiences.

Lean Thinking. Often (erroneously) described as "Lean Manufacturing," the Lean approach focuses on continually increasing customer value delivery while decreasing waste and inefficiency. Information about Lean principles can be found on the website of the Lean Enterprise Institute at www.lean.org, as well as in the book *Lean Thinking* by James P. Womack and Daniel T. Jones.

Six Sigma. The Six Sigma methodology focuses on improving processes by reducing or eliminating process variability. It differs from the Lean approach by focusing on improving existing processes rather than increasing value delivery, and on reducing defects rather than reducing waste and inefficiency. However, the two approaches are often combined into a single approach often referred to as **Lean Six Sigma**. Information about Six Sigma can be found at www.esixsigma.org and www.asq.org.

Toastmasters. The Toastmasters organization brings people together in almost every country on earth, working in local clubs to help people improve their speaking, listening, critical thinking, organization, and team-building skills. See their website at www.toastmasters.org. Most local Toastmasters clubs and Districts also have their own websites, where people can find a club near their home or work with a meeting time that works best for them.

UML. One of the best introductions to the Unified Modeling Language is the book *UML Distilled: Apply the Standard Object Modeling Language* by Martin Fowler and Kendall Scott. He explains not only the syntax of UML but the process behind how and why the different models are creating during application development.

"Working Toward". A lot of my inspiration for the concept of "Working Toward" and similar design concepts comes from Ann Lovejoy's *Handbook of Northwest Gardening*, one of the best books ever written on the art of gardening and landscape design. I recommend it to anyone with interest in landscape gardening, even if you don't live in the Northwest.

Abstraction. In Object-Oriented design, identifying the critical functionality that needs to be made available to the user.

AD. Agile Development.

Agile. An iterative approach to application (software) development, based on early and continuous delivery of working software.

Agile Model. A model owned and iteratively developed by an Agile team.

AK. Alternate Key. In a data model, the specification of a unique key or unique index that has not been chosen as the primary key or primary index.

Allies. People who can acquire resources, clear roadblocks, or resolve conflicts for a project team (or team member).

API. Application Programming Interface. This usually refers to a web service (or some similar service) that allows applications to interact with other applications, services, or databases.

Attribute. A characteristic or property of an entity in a logical data model.

AWS. Amazon Web Services. A cloud-based hosting site that provides computing and data storage resources for application developers.

BI. Business intelligence. The analysis and reporting of data in a way that allows the business to improve processes, create and strengthen stakeholder relationships, and recognize and take advantage of new and changing market conditions.

BDUF. Big Design Up Front. Refers to the creation of a large number of analysis and design artifacts at the beginning of a development project before any actual coding begins.

BPM. Business Process Management. Often used as a synonym for Business Process Reengineering.

BPR. Business Process Reengineering. The work of understanding an organization's end-to-end business process and refactoring it for greater efficiency.

CDM. Canonical Data Model. An Enterprise-level data model that can be used to interpret the data requirements of disparate applications and services, and thus connect them together.

CDM. See Canonical Data Model.

CEP. Complex Event Processing. The use of real-time (streaming) data analytics to determine the appropriate response to system events as they occur.

CI/CD. Continuous Integration and Continuous Deployment. Refers to the ability of software teams to deploy applications automatically from a central repository, enabling multiple updates of an application per day.

Cloud. A remote server environment in which computing, data storage, data processing, and application processing resources can be instantly allocated and scaled out according to resource need.

Cohesion. In Object-Oriented design, this refers to the organization of a set of related functions within a single module, rather than having them spread across multiple modules. The idea is that you should only have to go to one place to do anything related to that set of functions.

COMN. Common and Object Modeling Notation. An object-based approach to data modeling.

Conceptual Data Model. A high-level, business-focused data model aimed at obtaining business understanding and approval of the basic entities and relationships in the model.

COTS. Commercial, Off-the-Shelf Software. Applications that can be purchased, installed, and configured to an organization's need. SAP and Microsoft CRM are examples of COTS software.

Coupling. In Object-Oriented design, this refers to the degree of interdependence between separate modules; specifically, whether a change to any one module will cause functionality in another module to break.

CRM. Customer Relationship Management. The process of understanding and improving a company's relationships with its customer stakeholders.

CSV. Comma-Separated Values. A file-based data storage format where the individual data fields on each row are separated by commas.

Data Lake. A centralized but mostly unorganized collection of structured and unstructured data. Data lakes are used primarily for data persistence.

Data Model Scorecard. In Steve Hoberman's book *Data Modeling Made Simple*, a technique for assessing the quality and correctness of a data model.

Data Warehouse. An integrated store of data that supports BI and analytics processes. Data warehouses relate to the enterprise in scope, are historical (rather than real-time), conform to a defined schema (rather than containing raw data), and are normalized in structure (rather than aggregated).

DBA. Database Administrator; alternatively, Database Analyst.

DBMS. Database Management System. The software that enables users and applications to interact with databases.

DDD. Domain-Driven Development. An approach to software development that rejects the idea of databases being used to integrate applications or services, and advocates domain-specific persistence stores for related sets of application functions or services.

DDL. Data Definition Language. The SQL-based code used to create, alter and delete tables, views and other database objects.

Design Pattern. A general, reusable solution to a commonly occurring problem.

Design Thinking. An approach to problem solving in which Design is done (or at least considered) at the same time as requirements-gathering, and Designers are an integral part of the project team.

DevOps. A type of Agile development process characterized by multiple application deployments per day. Changes are often deployed directly into Production from the Development environment, after an initial "smoke test" has been successfully run.

DFD. Data Flow Diagram. A model showing the association between business process flows and their associated data stores.

DM. Data Management. The general field of all activities related to the design, creation, and management of data.

DMBOK. The Data Management Body of Knowledge; a compendium of information and best practices in data and information management.

DoD. Domain of Discourse, synonymous with "UoD" or "Universe of Discourse". A subset of the real world about which we make assertions.

Domain Model. A data model within which all business terms are consistently defined and understood. In this book, I equate a Domain Model with a Business Subject Area data model.

DQM. Data Quality Management. The business function of ensuring the highest quality of business data and its associated metadata.

EAI. Enterprise Application Integration. The use of services (including web and application services) to integrate applications together. See ESB.

EDW. Enterprise Data Warehouse. See "Data Warehouse".

EIM. Enterprise Information Management. The collection of best practices for effectively managing data assets across an enterprise or organization.

Encapsulation. In Object-Oriented design, the technique of hiding the complexity of a solution from the user and making a function easy to use.

Entity. A business object (such as Customer or Product), as represented in a logical data model.

ERD or E-R. Entity-Relational Diagram. A data modeling technique based on relationships between data entities and their attributes.

ERP. Enterprise Resource Planning. A type of COTS software used to manage high-level business functions such as accounting, payroll, human resources, manufacturing, etc. SAP and Baan are examples of ERP software.

ESB. Enterprise Service Bus. Software that controls the routing of messages between web services in a Service-Oriented Architecture (see SOA).

Essential Model. In David Hay's book *Achieving Buzzword Compliance*, an Essential Model ties together individual Semantic Models in a way that makes sense in the context of the high-level business constructs contained in the Overview Model.

FK. Foreign Key. In a data model, the association between attributes of a Child Entity and the primary key (PK) of a Parent Entity.

GHG. Greenhouse Gas, referring to the regulatory reporting of Greenhouse Gas emissions to various government regulatory agencies.

Hadoop. Java-based software that supports the distributed processing and analysis of very large data sets across multiple processing nodes.

HCD. Human-Centered Design. An approach to design thinking based on observation of how people experience a problem and attempt to solve it. In HCD, designers work empathetically and iteratively with people to help them find a solution that works for them.

IDEO. An organization that does design consulting for businesses and charitable organizations, using the principles of design thinking and Human-Centered Design. See www.ideo.org.

IT. Information Technology. The principal job of an IT organization is to facilitate, improve, and sustain enterprise-wide data and information processes.

JSON. JavaScript Object Notation. A Java-based data interchange and document format, similar to XML, used to transfer data between applications/services.

Kanban. A popular framework used to implement Agile and DevOps software development. It requires real-time communication of capacity and full transparency of work. Work items are represented visually on a board, allowing team members to see the state of every piece of work at any time.

LDM. Logical Data Model. In my books, a logical data model captures some Domain of the business, including business data definitions, rules, and constraints. It is used for getting agreement on business data requirements and communicating them to business and IT stakeholders.

Lean. A software development methodology based on principles of Lean Manufacturing.

MDM. Master Data Management. The process of creating and maintaining Enterprise-level core data entities and attributes that provide context to business processes and application transactions.

Metadata. Information about the characteristic properties of a data object or structure, usually contained within that object or structure. As used in this book, it also refers to information needed to help a business user assess the potential value or risk of a given set of data.

Model. In general terms, a model is an artifact used to gather and reach agreement on the requirements for the solution of a problem, and to implement some part of that solution.

MongoDB. A type of NoSQL database used mainly for document storage and retrieval.

MVC. Model-View-Controller. A popular application design pattern. The Model defines the data properties; the View defines the user interface; and the Controller defines the application functionality.

NoSQL. A data storage and processing solution not based on relational database technology. Relational databases are based on the concept of "schema on write"; data must be predefined before it can be stored. NoSQL databases are based on the concept of "schema on read"; data can be stored without being predefined, but is put into a defined form at the time it is retrieved.

Object-Relational. Refers to the disjunct between an application object's

Impedance Mismatch. view of data and the schema of the underlying relational database.

ODS. Operational Data Store. A type of Data Lake used to store data for the purpose of supporting application or service integration.

OEM. Original Equipment Manufacturer. In general terms, a company that provides branded parts, products, or services to customers.

OLTP. Online Transactional Processing. The day-to-day operational processes of an IT organization.

ORM. Object-Role Modeling. A type of conceptual data modeling in which attributes are treated as elementary facts and modeled as relationships.

ORM. Object-Relational Mapping. A type of application object class that maps a view of data to a set of relational database tables.

Overview Model. In David Hay's book *Achieving Buzzword Compliance*, an Overview Model contains the unified business ontology (similar to a Conceptual Data Model) that ties together the individual Semantic Models.

POC. Proof of Concept. A small-scale implementation of a new technology or business capability intended to identify the most workable approach or solution to a given problem.

PDM. Physical Data Model. Also called Physical Data Design. In my books, this is the mapping of some subset of the logical data model to an appropriate choice of architecture and technology, to support one or more applications or uses of data.

PK. Primary Key. In a relational data model (ERD), the set of attributes that ensures the uniqueness of each instance of an Entity.

PRISM. My acronym for five essential principles of physical data design: **P**erformance, **R**eusability, **I**ntegrity, **S**ecurity, and **M**aintainability.

QA. Quality Assurance. Work done to ensure that the delivered product meets the customer's requirements and expectations.

RDBMS. Relational Database Management System. Software that supports the creation and use of relational databases.

Refactor. To improve an application or database object without changing its behavior.

ROI. Return on Investment. What IT and BI expenditures are supposed to deliver and oftentimes don't.

SCRUM. A software development methodology based on Agile principles, characterized by organizing work into a "Product Backlog" and then performing the work in two- or three-week Sprints, followed by a post-Sprint review.

Semantic Model. In David Hay's book *Achieving Buzzword Compliance*, a Semantic Model contains business unit-specific divergences from the Overview Model, and correspond to Sub-Domain Models.

Set Theory. In mathematics, the formalized study of the relationships between sets (groups) of objects; set theory provides the mathematical basis for relational databases.

SOA. Service-Oriented Architecture. An architecture that allows applications and databases to interact through the medium of a web services "hub," rather than communicating directly.

Spike. A task within an Agile Sprint during which a prototype of a proposed solution to a problem will be developed and tested; this is R&D activity that takes place when the solution to a problem is not known, or when a choice must be made between two or more possible solutions.

Sprint. In the Scrum approach to Agile, one iteration of a development project.

SQL. Structured Query Language.Used to create objects and to query and manipulate data in relational databases.

SME. Subject matter expert. A business or IT person with advanced knowledge of a particular application or business process.

SSIS. SQL Server Integration Services. Despite the name, this has nothing to do with Microsoft SQL Server. SSIS is a general solution for migrating, transporting, and integrating data across multiple platforms.

Stakeholder. A party having a vested interest in the success or failure of an enterprise.

Sub-Domain Model. A subtype of a Domain Model containing entities and attributes specific to a particular business unit or business process.

TANSTAAFL. Acronym for "There Ain't No Such Thing As A Free Lunch", meaning that there are intrinsic costs associated with every economic choice.

TCO. Total Cost of Ownership. The sum total of initial investment, development, and maintenance over time for an IT application or database. This should never exceed the value it provides to the organization.

UDP. User-Defined Property. Most modeling tools give the user the ability to define customized properties for Entities, Attributes, Relationships, etc.

UML. Unified Modeling Language. An object-based modeling notation used to describe object classes and their components and relationships.

User Story. Also called Use Case. In Agile methodology, the description of a user requirement, usually of the form: "As a <role>, I want to do <description of task> so that <description of value generated>".

VDL. Virtual Data Layer. In my books, the VDL is a layer of virtual objects (such as database views, stored procedures, and user-defined functions) that provide a buffer between a data consumer's view of data and the schema of the underlying database (or persistence store). The VDL insulates data consumers from changes made to the database schema. I use the VDL to manage the Object-Relational Impedance Mismatch (see separate entry).

XML. Extensible Markup Language. A way of transmitting and/or storing data in text form.

XSLT. Extensible Stylesheet Language Transformations. An XML-based language for transforming or reformatting XML documents.

XP. Short for Extreme Programming. An approach to Agile software development in which pairs of programmers work together to continuously develop and refactor application code.

Zachman Framework   A logical schema for classifying Enterprise-level processes used to achieve consensus on requirements and develop models used to communicate those requirements between groups of stakeholders.

Lightning Source UK Ltd.
Milton Keynes UK
UKHW031624260722
406402UK00007B/1730

9 781634 629492